THE ASTD LEARNING AND
PERFORMANCE WORKBOOK SERIES

RAPID
Evaluation

**Tools, Worksheets, and
Job Aids to Help You:**

- **Develop an Evaluation
  Strategy**

- **Use the Right Evaluation
  Approach**

- **Understand and Analyze
  Evaluation Data**

ASTD
*Linking People,
Learning & Performance*

Susan Barksdale and Teri Lund

Ordering information: Books published by ASTD can be ordered by calling 800.628.2783 or 703.683.8100, or via the Web site at www.astd.org.

Library of Congress Catalog Card Number: 2001087844

ISBN:1-56286-287-1

Contents

Evaluation is a key business practice in learning and performance. An evaluation study will not only tell you where you've been and the results of your actions, it also will identify where you need to go in the future and identify the desired results of your future actions.

Over $1 trillion was spent on education and training in the United States in 1999 (*Forbes,* May 15, 2000). It is therefore no wonder that evaluation has increased in popularity with both workplace learning and performance (WLP) practitioners and their business partners. This rise in popularity is directly related to the need for both parties to accurately assess if a learning and performance intervention was worth the money and how it affects customers, learning, business processes and practices, and the bottom line.

In today's business environment, where increased competition and scarce resources prevail, organizations place value on learning and performance interventions that will yield the greatest results. Evaluation is not only accepted, but frequently requested. But how is this evaluation done? What works, and what doesn't work? How will you know if the effort you are putting into evaluation will provide you with the information needed?

Even though the need for evaluation has been acknowledged and many organizations have implemented some form of evaluation, it has not been universally embraced by WLP practitioners or their business partners. Evaluation often is viewed as a practice that takes too long to be meaningful and as an additional expense that cannot be justified. It is seen as a difficult practice that may not be supported by management and may not be worth the effort. Often it is threatening to WLP practitioners, who may fear negative results. Interestingly, according to the *ASTD 2000 State of the Industry Report* (ASTD, 2000), only 9 percent of industry leaders and 3 percent of ASTD Benchmarking Forum participants engaged in any form of Level 4 (Results) evaluation.

One of the main reasons these negative perceptions exist is that evaluation is often approached inconsis-

tently, with no grand plan in mind. Some organizations do evaluation when it "feels like a good thing to do" without following pre-established criteria that identify the what, when, who, and how of evaluation. Consequently, evaluation may be perceived as difficult because an accepted process is not used and methods and tools from one evaluation project are not transferred to another. This results in redundancy, re-work, increased costs, and frustration. The need for and ways to develop an evaluation strategy are topics that are not addressed in most of the WLP literature. But when considering the topics that are important for WLP professionals, it is obvious that evaluation is at the top of the list.

We have worked in the WLP field for a combined total of 40 years and have spent much of that time focused on how to make the results of our efforts more meaningful. Frustration over not always getting the results that we expected, or for that matter what our clients expected, led us to our interest in evaluation. What was a budding curiosity a decade and a half ago developed into a passion and then a structured approach to evaluation that is used by our WLP clients throughout the world.

This did not come easily. As those of you interested and involved in evaluation know, what seems simple at first glance is often complicated, both in practice and in the politics involved. Often what is complicated is determining if evaluation is needed and, if so, how to approach it.

We conceived our notion of strategic evaluation after engaging in several evaluation projects that started one way, shifted directions, and ended completely differently than what was anticipated. Positioning evaluation strategically versus tactically has made its implementation less complicated for our clients and has helped them plan for and deal with the people and politics involved.

Although we understand evaluation from its theoretical roots, this book reflects our education in "the school of hard knocks." It is the end result of our work over many years with numerous WLP clients to help them increase the quality of their deliverables and ensure their continued credible presence within the organization. We were encouraged by our clients and by those who have attended our public workshops to document this experience and provide a how-to book that would go beyond theory.

Think of this book as a guided tour of evaluation led by two people who have been on the evaluation front line and who have learned from their successes as well as their failures. This book reflects what we have learned, and we sincerely believe the evaluation processes, methods, and tools we provide will help you meet your evaluation needs.

Susan Barksdale and Teri Lund
May 2001

References

American Society for Training & Development. *The ASTD 2000 State of the Industry Report.* Alexandria, VA: ASTD, 2000.
The Informer. *Forbes,* May 15, 2000.

Introduction

The purpose of *Rapid Evaluation* is to provide you with a process and tools to get to evaluation results and deliver your message to those who need to understand it as quickly as possible. Whether you are responsible for evaluating all WLP interventions in your organization or specific interventions on a case-by-case basis, approaching evaluation in a strategic manner will help you link more effectively to your business partners' goals, strategies, and performance indicators. A strategic approach ultimately will provide them with the information they need and help them make informed decisions about the future use of WLP products and services.

You can use this workbook to guide a comprehensive organizational evaluation strategy, or you can use only the parts that apply to your specific evaluation needs at a given moment in time. For example, if you are in the middle of a Level 3 evaluation, you can consult chapter 6—Developing Level 3 (Behavior/ Transfer) Tools, which can help you conduct that level of evaluation. Appendix A, located at the end of this workbook, will help you quickly find the specific tools you need from among the more than 100 tools presented.

Rapid Evaluation provides the most up-to-date, proven evaluation techniques; it makes specific methods, case examples, checklists, and other tools available for immediate application to your organization. This workbook will show you how to

- identify the need for and purpose of an evaluation strategy
- develop an evaluation strategy
- determine a measurement approach
- align measures with the evaluation strategy
- communicate and gain commitment to the evaluation strategy
- determine if Level 1 evaluation is needed
- develop Level 1 tools
- determine if Level 2 evaluation is needed
- develop Level 2 tools

- determine if Level 3 evaluation is needed
- develop Level 3 tools
- determine if Level 4 evaluation is needed
- develop Level 4 tools
- determine if other tools (benchmarking, comprehensive review, or audit) are needed
- develop other tools
- pilot evaluation tools
- implement evaluation tools and collect data
- analyze the data collected
- make conclusions and recommendations and take the next steps
- maintain the evaluation strategy.

How *Rapid Evaluation* Is Different

So what about this workbook is different from others that are available? This one begins by helping you focus on your goals and what you need to evaluate. One reason evaluation is seen as a drawn-out and useless exercise is that professionals often engage in the wrong phase of evaluation. For example, let's say that the evaluation need is to determine the financial value of the program, but the evaluation project uses a reaction sheet that doesn't assess financial results. Or the need is to determine if facilities are adequate, but a testing strategy on the course's content is developed. Frequently what is evaluated does not meet the organization's need, and therefore the results are meaningless. This workbook can help you avoid such mistakes.

Rapid Evaluation also is different because it helps you determine where time and effort are best allocated and then provides tools to quickly identify the appropriate measures. In the recognition that "one size" of evaluation does not fit all needs, we have provided tools to use at varying levels of intensity. For example, a low-intensity evaluation using a Level 1 reaction sheet would be adequate for a one-time training event, whereas an ongoing high-intensity evaluation at Level 3 (Behavior/Transfer) would be required for a leadership development program. These tools ensure that your evaluation uses available resources in the best way to provide the information you need.

Target Audiences

WLP practitioners such as trainers, instructional designers, organizational development consultants, and human performance technologists will find this workbook most valuable. Managers in a variety of industries who are interested in or responsible for the effectiveness of WLP interventions may also find this book useful.

If your job involves improving human performance and you are interested in evaluating the effectiveness of workplace learning and performance in a practical and effective manner, then *Rapid Evaluation* is important reading for you.

Structure of the Book

This book consists of 13 chapters that relate directly to the steps in the evaluation process.

Chapter 1: Determining the Evaluation Strategy

In chapter 1, the need for and purpose of an evaluation strategy and how to develop one are addressed. The importance of identifying the purpose, objectives, focus, business linkage, structure, and expected results and resources is discussed, as well as linking an evaluation strategy to other key WLP processes.

Chapter 2: Establishing Measures

How to establish measures to use in evaluating a WLP strategy or intervention is introduced in chapter 2. Methods for validating business drivers and performance needs and linking them to measures are introduced, as well as ways to determine the level of intensity for the evaluation. Aligning measures with the objectives of an evaluation strategy or intervention also is addressed.

Chapter 3: Communicating and Gaining Commitment to the Strategy

In chapter 3, the focus is on how to communicate the need for an evaluation strategy and how to influence others to gain their commitment to developing and implementing the strategy. A communication process

and plan are introduced, and the basic principles for influencing a commitment are outlined.

Chapter 4: Developing Level 1 (Reaction) Tools

Level 1 evaluation is defined in this chapter, along with the criteria for when to use it. The data components for Level 1 are identified and a process introduced for how to develop tools to evaluate at this level. The characteristics of low-, moderate-, and high-intensity measurements for Level 1 are described.

Chapter 5: Developing Level 2 (Learning) Tools

In chapter 5, Level 2 evaluation is defined and the criteria for when to evaluate at this level outlined. The different types of learning assessments are addressed, along with the relationship of Bloom's taxonomy to Level 2 evaluation. Building Level 2 tools at low, moderate, and high intensities is included in this step.

Chapter 6: Developing Level 3 (Behavior/Transfer) Tools

This chapter defines Level 3 evaluation and identifies when to use it. It addresses how to ensure that you have a set of balanced measures that will provide the right information to decision makers. The importance of baselining and how to measure a baseline are presented. Building Level 3 tools at low, moderate, and high intensities is included in chapter 6.

Chapter 7: Developing Level 4 (Results) Tools

Evaluating at Level 4 is defined in this chapter and when to use it identified. The levels of intensity for a Level 4 evaluation are introduced, and how to build tools at low, moderate, and high intensity is described.

Chapter 8: Developing Other Tools

Chapter 8 addresses when to use tools other than those for Levels 1 to 4 to evaluate WLP strategies and interventions. How to determine the need for these other tools and how to develop them are included in this step, and tools are provided for benchmarking, comprehensive review, and audits.

Chapter 9: Piloting the Tools

The focus of chapter 9 is on piloting evaluation tools, including how to plan the pilot and identify who is responsible for the various pilot actions. Also included in this chapter is how to communicate the results of the pilot and how to determine the priority of the identified changes.

Chapter 10: Implementing the Tools and Collecting Data

Chapter 10 addresses how to implement the tools used to collect the data for an evaluation strategy or intervention, including how to communicate the implementation and ensure the quality of the data.

Chapter 11: Analyzing the Data

How to analyze the data collected from using the evaluation tools developed in chapters 4 through 8 is introduced in this chapter and an analysis process described. Definitions of the data analysis methods most commonly used to analyze evaluation data are provided, and the importance of documenting data bias and inconsistency is addressed.

Chapter 12: Making Conclusions and Recommendations and Taking the Next Steps

Chapter 12 addresses how to document the conclusions and recommendations and take the next steps following your analysis of the evaluation data. Linking conclusions and recommendations back to the business need is highlighted in this chapter.

Chapter 13: Maintaining the Evaluation Strategy

Maintaining an evaluation strategy is the final step of the process. How to identify internal and external changes that trigger the need for maintenance, how to review organizational changes and their impact on the strategy, and the questions to ask to determine the needed changes are all discussed in this chapter.

In addition to the 13 chapters relating to each step of the evaluation process, this workbook contains appendixes that provide an index of the evaluation tools presented, a glossary of evaluation terms, and a listing of additional evaluation references.

Using the processes, case examples, and tools presented in this workbook, you should be able to develop a comprehensive evaluation strategy, communicate it, and gain commitment to it. You should also be able to identify meaningful measures based on business drivers, business needs, and performance needs.

It is expected that you will be able to identify the level of evaluation that will be most appropriate for your organization or for specific interventions and to create tools of varying intensity for each of these levels. Recognizing that not all evaluation fits the framework of Kirkpatrick's four levels, you should also be able to identify when additional tools are needed and develop them.

Further, you should be able to conduct a pilot for the evaluation tools you have developed and work through the entire process of implementing and collecting the data resulting from the tools, analyze the data using the most appropriate analysis method, and arrive at conclusions and recommendations. Finally, you should also be able to maintain the strategy you have developed so that it becomes a living document.

The ASTD Learning and Performance Workbook Series

Rapid Evaluation is the first book in the ASTD Learning and Performance Workbook Series, which is designed to provide WLP practitioners with a foundation for the practices that are at the core of our profession. Much like this book, each workbook consists of a practical, step-by-step process and useful tools. The series will also address such topics as needs analysis, strategic planning, and competency development.

You can use these workbooks individually to focus on a specific WLP practice, or they can be used together to provide a comprehensive overview of the practices that are most important to WLP. In any event, we are certain that you will benefit from the concepts, practices, and tools presented in this workbook and that you will be able to apply them to your work.

Determining the Evaluation Strategy

To help you ensure that evaluation and its results are welcomed and acted on, this chapter discusses tools and techniques for creating an effective evaluation strategy. An evaluation strategy can serve as a guideline and source for all evaluation efforts within an organization, and this chapter will help you create such a strategy. An evaluation strategy can also relate to a specific intervention or project, and the last section in this chapter discusses the similarities and differences between the evaluation strategies for a specific intervention versus an entire organization. The following topics are discussed in this chapter:

- need for and purposes of an organizational evaluation strategy
- benefits of developing and using an evaluation strategy
- case examples illustrating the development and use of evaluation strategies
- identifying evaluation strategy components and methods
- determining the focus of the evaluation strategy
- linking evaluation to business needs
- determining the scope of the evaluation strategy
- structuring the evaluation strategy
- identifying expected results
- identifying the resources required to implement the evaluation strategy
- integrating with other processes
- identifying reporting requirements
- documenting the strategy
- determining an evaluation strategy for a specific intervention.

Need for an Evaluation Strategy

Although evaluation is usually advantageous, many workplace learning and performance (WLP) professionals are uncertain whether to pursue it. You can use worksheet 1.1 individually or in a group to reflect on and discuss the need for an evaluation strategy. This tool will help you determine if evaluation is critical to your or your client's organization. Read each statement listed in the right-hand column. If the statement is a critical factor to the organization, place a checkmark in the "yes" column. If the statement is not critical, then place a checkmark in the "no" column. Count the number of "yes" checkmarks. If you have three or more, then the organization's interventions, solutions, products, and services are strong candidates for evaluation.

We use the terms *solution* and *performance solution* throughout the book to refer to a corrective action or product put in place to remedy a performance problem or need. In our profession, examples of solutions are courseware, e-learning, electronic performance support systems, job aids, or change to or addition of a process.

Benefits of an Evaluation Strategy

You and your organization can realize important benefits from an organizational evaluation strategy. An evaluation strategy

- assists in organizing the continuous improvement process
- establishes priorities by linking products and services to business objectives
- reduces time-consuming struggles in ensuring that results are tracked

Worksheet 1.1: Is There a Need for Evaluation?

Yes	No	Is this critical to you or your organization?
☐	☐	Is it important for you to know if your customers think your services and products are valuable?
☐	☐	Do you need to know if your services and products are used back on the job?
☐	☐	Is it important to determine how your services and products could be improved?
☐	☐	Do you need to provide performance feedback to those who provide the services and products?
☐	☐	Is it important to identify new needs for those who use the services and products so that you can enhance the services or products you offer or develop new ones?
☐	☐	Do you need to know if the dollars invested in a product or service resulted in a payback for the customer or the organization?
☐	☐	Do you need to link the products and services directly to the business and determine if they contributed to business goals?
☐	☐	Do you need to assess if the products and services and the mechanisms for delivering them meet or exceed best practices?
☐	☐	Is it important to determine if a product or service is meeting its established objectives?
☐	☐	Are you interested in collecting data for marketing or as a baseline for decision making for future programs or solutions?
☐	☐	Do you need to provide the test results of participants who are using a product for accreditation, certification, regulation, or other purpose?
☐	☐	Do you need to determine if the products and services increased the organization's intellectual capital or improved employees' ability to manage the organization's knowledge?

- ensures that the quality and quantity of data gathered facilitate decision making and that efforts to capture data are not wasted
- forces evaluation to be a *process* and not an *event*
- integrates evaluation into analysis, design, and development, ensuring a results-oriented product or service.

Case Examples

Every organization is different. Consequently, the incentives and needs for evaluating are unique for each organization. The following case examples illustrate the evaluation strategy approaches of three very different organizations.

Case Example 1

Superior Training Group is a large training delivery organization that needs to gather more sophisticated data about its customers, who are outside the company, and the customers' satisfaction levels with the company's services and products, for which they pay fees of $1,000 to $10,000.

The services and products the company offers include

- classroom instruction (including laboratories and hands-on experiences)
- electronic performance support systems (EPSSs)
- help desks
- Web-based training.

The intent of the company's services and products is to reduce errors by its customers' staffs, reduce time to proficiency for the customers' employees, reduce rework, and increase the customer's ability to solve equipment operating problems internally rather than relying on expensive external solutions.

Superior determined that the evaluation strategy for its business would consist of five elements:

1. a standard online questionnaire of five key questions focusing on future needs, satisfaction with the product or service used, ease of acquisition of the service or product used, customer demographics, and likelihood of using other products offered by Superior
2. a 25-question online or paper survey that could be used randomly or when problems surfaced and that asked more in-depth performance

management questions about the resources delivering or supporting the product or service and satisfaction with the logistics or media of the service or product; the survey could be customized by selecting three to five items to address a specific product, service, or problem

3. a reporting system for the testing Superior does in certifying and accrediting its customers

4. methods to estimate return-on-investment (ROI) for the management of Superior's customer companies

5. a reporting system that could produce standard reports for the customer's management and Superior's personnel and had limited ad hoc reporting capability

These requirements drove an evaluation strategy comprising the following components:

- Level 1 (Reaction) data gathering and reporting
- Level 2 (Learning) validation of instruments used, data gathering, and reporting
- Level 4 (Results) low-intensity tracking system for customer ROI
- a standard and ad hoc reporting system accessible to both the customer and Superior.

Case Example 2

Creative Solutions has offices located throughout the world. It offers WLP products and services globally to internal customers only, using both outside providers and internal staff members. It needs to ensure that the quality of its WLP products and services is consistent regardless of provider or method. The other key driver in Creative's strategy is to determine which products and services provide knowledge building or skill development that is actually used back on the job.

These requirements drove an evaluation strategy comprising the following components:

- Level 1 (Reaction) data gathering and reporting
- performance monitoring evaluation tools (instructor evaluations, peer assessments, and subject matter expert, or SME, evaluations)
- Level 3 (Behavior/Transfer) medium-intensity tracking system for transfer to the job.

Case Example 3

ABC Training Co. designs and delivers a variety of training interventions using primarily classroom or Web-based delivery media. However, the products and interventions need to be designed and delivered consistently. In addition, management believes that the group designing and delivering the interventions needs to be best in class to provide a product that creates best-in-class skills in intervention participants.

These requirements drove an evaluation strategy with the following components:

- benchmarking data collection of best-in-class WLP design and delivery organizations to establish standards and then measure ABC's knowledge, skills, products, and services against those standards
- Level 1 (Reaction) data gathering and reporting
- Level 2 (Learning) validation of instruments used, data gathering, and reporting
- Level 3 (Behavior/Transfer) low-intensity tracking system for transfer to the job.

Purpose and Objectives of an Evaluation Strategy

The purpose of an evaluation strategy is to provide you and your stakeholders with a clear vision of what you want evaluation to accomplish for your performance improvement solutions, products, and services. In other words, what information do you need about how customers and clients perceive and use the products and services you provide and the results realized from them? Evaluation is simply a quality control methodology, and the evaluation strategy assists in being clear up front about what information you need to be able to determine if the products and services you provide are effective and efficient and how they can be improved.

Understanding the need for evaluation and what you (and your sponsor, business partners, and customers) expect the evaluation components to provide is critical in designing your evaluation strategy. The need for evaluation defines the purpose. We suggest you use the questions in worksheet 1.1 to establish a dialog with your sponsor, stakeholders, and business partners to determine what the need for evaluation is and, consequently, what your purpose for evaluation should be.

Once you have had a dialog with your sponsor and other key parties regarding the need for the evaluation strategy, you should be able to develop a one- to three-statement paragraph that defines the purpose of the evaluation strategy. Three examples of evaluation strategy purpose statements are as follows:

1. The purpose of the evaluation strategy is to provide the Planning and Development Department with clear information regarding our clients' certification status and how, once they are certified, the certification education provides clients results back on the job.

2. The purpose of the evaluation strategy is to provide Education Services with information reflecting customer perceptions of the usefulness and quality of our products. The strategy should also serve as a mini-needs analysis about our customers' future needs.

3. The purpose of the evaluation strategy is to compare our services and products against those in the field that are seen as best in class. The strategy also will assist us in determining what changes are needed in our processes and tools so we are perceived as best in class by the competition and our customers.

As you can see, the evaluation strategy purpose can be very different from organization to organization. It should define what will be accomplished through implementing an evaluation strategy in a clear statement that can be used to communicate and market the overall strategy and its specific components.

Once the purpose is defined, the next task is to develop the objectives for the evaluation strategy. Several actions may be required to meet the purpose, and these are defined in the objectives. Table 1.1 lists the purpose of an evaluation strategy related to strategy objectives. Each of the evaluation strategy purpose statements identified above is listed in the first column, and corresponding objectives are listed in the second column.

Worksheet 1.2 can help you summarize the purpose of the evaluation strategy and the objectives that you expect to accomplish through implementing specific evaluation tactics and components in your organization. Document what you think evaluation should accomplish in column 1. Then in column 2, identify the impact those accomplishments would have on your group. In column 3, identify the business result your customer would realize from the accomplishments. And finally, in column 4, identify what you think the payoff is for pursuing this type of evaluation for the organization as a whole. An example of how to complete this worksheet is provided in the first row.

Table 1.1: Sample Purpose Statements and Related Objectives

Evaluation Strategy Purpose Statement	Related Objective
The purpose of the evaluation strategy is to provide the Planning and Development Department with clear information regarding our clients' certification status and how, once they are certified, the certification education provides clients results back on the job.	To develop assessments (observations and tests) that can be used at the end of each training session to determine if the participants can perform the identified functions as predefined for the training session To develop a tool or survey to determine what results back on the job (if any) clients are seeing as a result of certification
The purpose of the evaluation strategy is to provide Education Services with information reflecting customer perceptions of the usefulness and quality of our products. The strategy should also serve as a mini-needs analysis about our customers' future needs.	To develop a survey for participants to determine what their perceptions are of the usefulness and quality of our products in comparison to others (specifically certain competitors) To develop a mechanism to gather information from the participants (while we have them as a captive audience) about what future training needs they will have in the short and long term
The purpose of the evaluation strategy is to compare our services and products against those in the field that are seen as best in class. The strategy also will assist us in determining what changes are needed in our processes and tools so we are perceived as best in class by the competition and our customers.	To identify who is seen as best in class in our profession and why To determine what those who are best in class have as processes and tools that contribute to their stellar performance To identify how we can change our processes or tools so we can duplicate best-in-class performance

Worksheet 1.2: Summarizing Your Evaluation Strategy

What Evaluation Should Accomplish	Evaluation's Impact on Your Group	Evaluation's Impact on Your Customer or Client	Evaluation's Payoff to the Organization as a Whole
Determine if courseware is effective and participants use the information back on the job	Provide information about how design influences or detracts from transfer to the job	Increased satisfaction with courseware that is useful and provides job results	Performance changes and business needs for training requests are met

Identifying Evaluation Strategy Components

Determining the components to include in an evaluation strategy is the first and key activity in developing an evaluation strategy. Look at the 20 evaluation statements in worksheet 1.3 and rank them on a scale of 3 to 0 by circling the number that applies to each statement. The statements given the highest rating (3) indicate the components most critical to include in your evaluation strategy. The following questions should be helpful in defining the purpose of your strategy, and taking the time to examine these questions now will help you avoid problems in future steps in your strategy:

- What information is critical for you to gather to address the driving factors?
- How will this information be gathered?
- How will the information-gathering method affect your overall strategy?

- How will you validate (i.e., confirm or corroborate) the driving factors?
- What benefits will this type of evaluation provide the department or organization?

Identifying Evaluation Methods

Once you have determined that an evaluation strategy is needed, you will need to identify an appropriate evaluation methodology. Definitions of the evaluation methods you should consider are provided to assist you in identifying the most effective ones for your organization's needs:

- *Benchmarking against best practices:* This evaluation practice involves gathering information about other companies' performance results and best practices and then comparing your organization's performance to that data.

Worksheet 1.3: Identifying Components of an Evaluation Strategy

Evaluation Statement	is a driving factor for my organization.	applies to my organization but is not a driving factor.	may apply to my organization.	is not applicable to my organization.
1. Our marketplace is continually increasing competitively.	3	2	1	0
2. We are using new media to deliver learning solutions to our users.	3	2	1	0
3. Our budget and resources, although increasing, are not meeting the demand of our customers.	3	2	1	0
4. Continuous improvement and process improvement are highly valued.	3	2	1	0
5. Demonstrating results is highly valued.	3	2	1	0
6. Management has mandated performance changes.	3	2	1	0
7. Management does not understand the purpose and value of performance improvement as a business strategy.	3	2	1	0
8. A new initiative or system is being implemented companywide.	3	2	1	0
9. Our business partners, customers, or managers are asking if there has been a business impact.	3	2	1	0
10. We need to differentiate our performance improvement solutions from others.	3	2	1	0
11. We need to quantify the instructional value of our exercises (e.g., classroom, CBT, Web-based courses, self-study).	3	2	1	0
12. We need to quantify if and when a participant's impressions change (e.g., early in course, after exercise).	3	2	1	0
13. We need to identify what motivates learners to change actions or behaviors.	3	2	1	0

Evaluation Statement	is a driving factor for my organization.	applies to my organization but is not a driving factor.	may apply to my organization.	is not applicable to my organization.
14. We need to quantify a performance gap.	3	2	1	0
15. We need a methodology to identify which medium to use in different cases.	3	2	1	0
16. We need to increase customer loyalty.	3	2	1	0
17. We need to measure employees' performance.	3	2	1	0
18. The organization considers customers' perspectives and knowledge of customers to be key to doing business.	3	2	1	0
19. Certification or performance management is prevalent throughout the organization.	3	2	1	0
20. New processes or methods of providing learning solutions have been introduced in my department.	3	2	1	0

Reprinted with permission from Barksdale, Susan B., and Lund, Teri B. *What Evaluation Approach Provides the Biggest Payoff? Team and Organization Sourcebook.* Edited by Mel Silberman. New York: McGraw-Hill, 2001.

- *Competitive research:* This evaluation method involves gathering information from competitors about their evaluation practices via literature searches or networking.

- *Audit of solution against standards:* This method of evaluation involves auditing a solution or training program to ensure that a process was followed or that pre-established criteria were met.

- *Kirkpatrick's four levels:* This universally accepted model for evaluating performance improvement interventions consists of four steps or levels (Kirkpatrick, 1994) Level 1 (Reaction) measures how participants react to the solution or intervention. Level 2 (Learning) measures the extent to which participants improve knowledge or increase skill as a result of the solution or intervention. Level 3 (Behavior/Transfer) measures whether behavior has changed back on the job as a result of the solution or intervention. Level 4 (Results) measures the impact the solution or intervention has had on the business and often includes ROI evaluation.

- *Balanced scorecard:* The balanced scorecard is a way for organizations to evaluate effectiveness beyond using financial measures only (Kaplan & Norton, 1996). The model consists of measuring effectiveness using four perspectives: 1) the customer perspective (did the solution, intervention, or practice meet the customer's need or expectation?), 2) the learning perspective (did the users gain the needed skills or knowledge?), 3) the business perspective (did the solution, intervention, or practice have an effect back on the job?), and 4) the financial perspective (did the solution, intervention, or practice have a financial payoff?). There is a similarity between Kirkpatrick's four levels and the balanced scorecard, but the balanced scorecard places more of a business emphasis on evaluating performance improvement interventions.

- *Performance audit:* This evaluation method tracks individual or organizational performance to plan. It can be done as part of a needs assessment or as part of an evaluation to see if transfer to the job has occurred and if individual or organizational performance has improved as expected.

- *Peer analysis:* In this type of evaluation peers use agreed-on criteria to evaluate each others'

work or results in order to identify strengths and opportunities for improvement.

- *Expert review:* This evaluation method uses SMEs to observe or review results to ensure credibility and accuracy.

- *Impact analysis:* This method consists of using leading indicators to predict or validate lagging indicators and identifying causes and effects.

- *Certification review:* This method of evaluation involves establishing certification criteria and measuring the extent to which a participant meets them.

Use the matrix in table 1.2 to identify the evaluation methods that might best be used to gather data to address the evaluation concerns you identified using worksheet 1.3.

Table 1.2: Evaluation Strategy Method Matrix

Evaluation Statement	Evaluation Method
1. Our marketplace is continually increasing competitively.	Benchmarking or best practices Competitive research
2. We are using new media to deliver learning solutions to our users.	Benchmarking or best practices Audit of solution against standards Kirkpatrick's four levels Balanced scorecard Performance audit
3. Our budget and resources, although increasing, are not meeting the demand of our customers.	Benchmarking or best practices Audit of solution against standards Kirkpatrick's four levels Balanced scorecard Performance audit
4. Continuous improvement and process improvement are highly valued.	Benchmarking or best practices Audit of solution against standards Kirkpatrick's four levels Balanced scorecard Peer analysis Expert review Impact analysis Performance audit Certification review

Evaluation Statement	Evaluation Method
5. Demonstrating results is highly valued.	Benchmarking or best practices Audit of solution against standards Kirkpatrick's four levels Balanced scorecard Peer analysis Expert review Performance audit Impact analysis
6. Management has mandated performance changes.	Benchmarking or best practices Audit of solution against standards Kirkpatrick's four levels Balanced scorecard Peer analysis Expert review Impact analysis Performance audit Certification review
7. Management does not understand the purpose and value of performance improvement as a business strategy.	Benchmarking or best practices Balanced scorecard Impact analysis
8. A new initiative or system is being implemented companywide.	Kirkpatrick's four levels Balanced scorecard Peer analysis Expert review Impact analysis Performance audit
9. Our business partners, customers, or managers are asking if there has been an impact on business.	Audit of solution against standards Kirkpatrick's four levels Balanced scorecard Peer analysis Expert review Impact analysis Performance audit Certification review
10. We need to differentiate our performance improvement solutions from others.	Benchmarking or best practices Audit of solution against standards Balanced scorecard Peer analysis Expert review Impact analysis Performance audit Certification review

(continued next page)

Table 1.2: Evaluation Strategy Method Matrix *(continued)*

Evaluation Statement	Evaluation Method
11. We need to quantify the instructional value of our exercises (e.g., classroom, CBT, Web-based courses, self-study).	Audit of solution against standards Kirkpatrick's four levels Balanced scorecard Performance audit Method review
12. We need to quantify if and when a participant's impressions change (e.g., early in course, after exercise).	Audit of solution against standards Kirkpatrick's four levels
13. We need to identify what motivates learners to change actions or behaviors.	Audit of solution against standards Performance audit
14. We need to quantify a performance gap.	Audit of solution against standards Kirkpatrick's four levels Balanced scorecard Impact analysis Performance audit Certification review
15. We need a methodology to identify which medium to use in different cases.	Audit of solution against standards Kirkpatrick's four levels Balanced scorecard Performance audit Method review
16. We need to increase customer loyalty.	Audit of solution against standards Kirkpatrick's four levels Balanced scorecard
17. We need to measure employees' performance.	Audit of solution against standards Kirkpatrick's four levels Balanced scorecard Impact analysis Performance audit Certification review
18. The organization considers customer perspective and knowledge of its customers to be key to doing business.	Kirkpatrick's four levels Balanced scorecard
19. Certification or performance management is prevalent throughout the organization.	Kirkpatrick's four levels Balanced scorecard Peer analysis Expert review Impact analysis Certification review

Evaluation Statement	Evaluation Method
20. New processes or methods of providing learning solutions have been introduced in my department.	Benchmarking or best practices Audit of solution against standards Kirkpatrick's four levels Balanced scorecard Peer analysis Expert review Impact analysis Certification review

Determining the Focus of the Evaluation Strategy

If you have had difficulty identifying the components of an evaluation strategy or in validating what components should be included, you should consider sharpening the focus of the evaluation strategy, or the nature of the entity the strategy has as its focal point. The focus of an evaluation strategy is extremely important in ensuring that the strategy will provide the correct tools to assess how the organization can change processes, specific project deliverables, services, and products that better meet business goals.

Answering the question—Who are the customers who will be affected by the evaluation strategy?—is helpful in focusing on what the evaluation strategy will provide and how. The answer to this question, which on the surface seems easy and obvious, often is convoluted. For example,

- Is the customer the manager of the employees who use the service or product?
- Is the customer the person who actually uses the service or product and whose performance is improved or knowledge increased?
- Is the customer the person or manager who "pays" for the product or service—for example, a senior manager or someone outside the company who approves the cost and is held accountable for the expenditure's outcomes?
- Is the customer internal? external?

It is possible to have several types of customers or several customers within one type, all with different needs. Table 1.3 illustrates the various levels of customers and their unique needs and desired outcomes for two interventions.

Customers' differing needs and desired outcomes are important to recognize and will influence the

Table 1.3: Determining Customers, Needs, and Desired Outcomes for Two Interventions

Intervention Example	Customer and Need	Desired Outcome
An electronic performance support system (EPSS) that provides detailed information via PC to support customer calls and inquiries regarding equipment problems	Primary customer • Manager needs time to proficiency reduced for new employees so they can take on calls earlier and provide same level of customer service as experienced employees. • Employees need to be able to answer questions from external customers in a minimal amount of time and within service contract goals to meet performance goals.	Reduced call time Correct and consistent responses to customers Increased confidence of the call center employee for taking call
	Secondary customer • External customer needs questions answered quickly, correctly, and consistently regardless of who responds to call.	Reduced wait and call time Correct information regardless of who answers call Resolution of equipment problem

(continued next page)

Table 1.3: Determining Customers, Needs, and Desired Outcomes for Two Interventions *(continued)*

Intervention Example	Customer and Need	Desired Outcome
A course offered via the Web and in the classroom that assists managers in developing or enhancing coaching skills and provides a process and tools to use when in a coaching situation with an employee	**Primary customer** • Manager needs assistance in coaching employees for performance improvement and career development. • Employees need coaching to improve performance and have requested coaching for career development.	Improved job performance Improved employee satisfaction with development opportunities Enhanced working relationships between employees and managers
	Secondary customer • Senior management needs managers that "walk the talk" and can assist employees in developing skills and knowledge levels for business operating requirements.	Higher skilled workforce and fewer performance problems Higher productivity Increased employee satisfaction

development of the evaluation strategy. For example, is it more important to the business goals of the organization that the external customer has a resolution to his or her problem, or is more important to ensure that the customer call center employees have a feeling of confidence and are more likely to stay in the job? The answer to this question will help you determine the focus of the evaluation strategy.

Obviously, customers and their needs will vary, but all too often WLP professionals try to limit their definitions of who constitutes a customer, believing that too many customers can get confusing. But the flip side is that by not looking at all the customers vying for your services, you may not meet critical performance needs. By defining each of your most important customers and identifying their roles, you can more clearly determine the focus of evaluation for the organization or for an intervention. Remember also that a single customer might have multiple roles. For example, an "employee" may also be a "paying customer" (e.g., the customer who pays out of his or her own pocket to attend a certification training class). Table 1.4 identifies four types of WLP customers and their associated evaluation requirements.

An integral part of focusing the evaluation strategy is to determine who are the most important customers for your products and services (in other words, who keeps you in business) and what information is needed to ensure that you are meeting their needs and retaining their business. In implementing an evaluation strategy, consider the following regarding your customers:

• Who are your customers, and what are the roles of each in relation to the products and services you offer?

• Why is each type of customer important to you?

• What information would be beneficial to you in providing better services or products to your customers?

• How do your customers define satisfaction with your products and services?

• If you could deliver satisfaction to only one customer, which customer would it be most important to satisfy?

• What is important to your customers, and how is this represented in the evaluation strategy?

Balancing the Evaluation

Too often (although understandably), WLP professionals think the most important evaluation perspective is that of the customer. It is not that the customer viewpoint is not valuable, but it alone does not always tell the whole story about the quality or success of WLP performance solutions, interventions, products, processes, or services. If you consider only the customer perspective, you will have a one-sided view. For instance, customers may be "very satisfied," but they take their new skills and knowledge to the competition, and the organization receives no benefit. Or the customer is "very dissatisfied," but you don't know why. Was the solution designed poorly? Is there an organizational problem beyond what you can resolve? Is the problem easy to fix, or is it difficult?

A balanced evaluation strategy helps you realize a more comprehensive assessment of what is working well, what needs adjustment, and what needs a com-

Table 1.4: Evaluation Strategy Customers

Customer	Role	Evaluation Requirement
Participants or users	The people who, back on the job, use the products and services being evaluated	Customer satisfaction Perception of service or product Usefulness of service or product Design of service or product Application of service or product
Funders	The person or group that funds use of the service or product	Customer satisfaction Return-on-investment Cost comparison
Manager of participants or users	The manager of the people who use the products or services	Customer satisfaction Perception of service or product Usefulness of service or product Design of service or product Application of service or product Time and cost comparison
WLP manager or sponsor	The WLP manager who manages the development, implementation, and ongoing processes that support the services and products offered	Customer satisfaction Perception of service or product Usefulness of service or product Design of service or product Application of service or product Competitive comparisons

plete overhaul. When the evaluation strategy is implemented, it should provide balanced information that tells you the following:

1. *the customer perspective:* whether the customer is satisfied, feels that his or her skills or knowledge has improved, and can perform at a higher level back on the job or has enhanced career opportunities

2. *the WLP perspective:* what you do well, what needs to be improved, and what is missing altogether

3. *the organizational perspective:* whether the desired benefits from the organizational perspective have been realized (e.g., workers have increased skills, knowledge is shared, return-on-investment is realized, performance problem is resolved, business objectives are met).

This balance is illustrated in figure 1.1.

By building an evaluation strategy that embraces a balanced approach, you can more effectively measure the quality of the intervention. The information from the evaluation will provide a clearer picture of the results and will thus inform more strategic decisions, moving WLP professionals to a more influential position as leaders rather than order takers.

Linking the Evaluation Strategy to Business Needs

The next thing you should consider in building an evaluation strategy is linking it to business needs. *Business needs* are what a business must do to be successful, such as increase its presence in the marketplace, identify high-potential employees, ensure that workers are sufficiently trained, or increase customer satisfaction. Failure to link to business needs is a fault that compromises not only an evaluation strategy but also the design of WLP services and products. There should be a clear link from business goal or objective to a specific intervention (figure 1.2).

If you are unable to make this link, then you need more information. A difficult obstacle in providing quality WLP products, services, and interventions is

Figure 1.1: A Balanced Evaluation Strategy

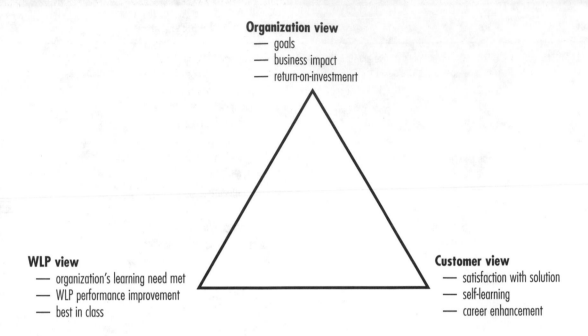

Organization view
— goals
— business impact
— return-on-investmenrt

WLP view
— organization's learning need met
— WLP performance improvement
— best in class

Customer view
— satisfaction with solution
— self-learning
— career enhancement

that business goals or priorities are not always easily identified, especially in today's rapidly changing and highly competitive environment. It is especially important to ask the key questions listed in table 1.5 as part of the evaluation strategy to ensure that products, services, and interventions are in alignment with the goals and priorities of the business. You can use these questions in a focus group or strategy work group or when interviewing senior managers.

Clearly, not all 10 questions need link to the evaluation strategy. However, if the strategy is not directly linked to business needs, it most likely will not provide management with information, products, and services that are key to its operation. Also, without this linkage, WLP is less likely to be seen as a leader and partner in human performance improvement.

Determining the Scope of the Strategy

The scope of the evaluation strategy involves what you will and will not evaluate, to what level of intensity,

Figure 1.2: Linking with the Business Need

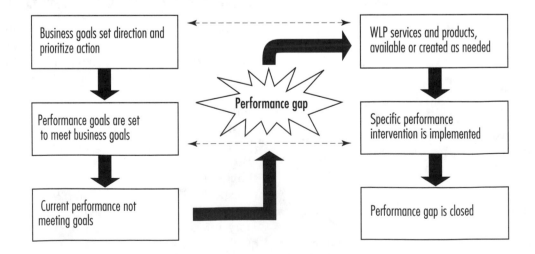

Business goals set direction and prioritize action

WLP services and products, available or created as needed

Performance goals are set to meet business goals

Performance gap

Specific performance intervention is implemented

Current performance not meeting goals

Performance gap is closed

Table 1.5: Business Linkage Questions

Question	Linkage to the Evaluation Strategy
What are the three biggest challenges that face this organization in the next one to three years?	Will the evaluation strategy provide information about the organization's ability to meet those challenges? For example, the evaluation strategy provides information on individual performance gaps. Will the evaluation strategy identify potential weaknesses or vulnerabilities regarding the challenges? For example, the evaluation strategy provides performance trends and tracks performance change against goals.
What is the organization doing to respond to those challenges?	Is the evaluation strategy flexible, allowing for changes to occur in the organization as a result of its need to meet new challenges? For example, the evaluation strategy is not tied to a specific method, but rather objectives, and if the media change it can still evaluate the effectiveness of an intervention.
What information is most important to communicate today to the employees of the organization? Is it being communicated accurately and fully?	Is the evaluation strategy in alignment with this type of information? For example, cost information is most important, and the evaluation strategy tracks cost comparisons and financial results.
What are the most important results to be achieved this year, next year, and three years from now?	Does the evaluation strategy track against the results and provide support information for them? For example, sales are the most important result, and the evaluation strategy tracks sales training or other types of sales support and its results.
If you were in charge of evaluation and quality management for WLP, what do you think would be the most important things to measure?	Is the evaluation strategy linked to the measures management thinks are most valuable? For example, management thinks having an impact back on the job is more important than test results, so that is demonstrated in the strategy.
What type of evaluation information regarding individuals' learning and performance would be most valuable to the business today?	This is a check question to ensure the strategy is linked to the measures management thinks are of greatest value.
When viewing learning and performance capacity, what are our strengths and weaknesses as an organization?	Does the evaluation strategy provide information in alignment with the strengths and weaknesses of the organization? For example, management sees team support as a performance capacity issue, and the evaluation strategy reports indicators of how individuals work together or communicate with each other post-training.
What changes do you expect may happen that could have pivotal organizational impact? In what way would the changes affect the organization?	Is the evaluation strategy flexible, and can the strategy be realigned as changes occur? For example, the key products and services are sales programs but there is a shift to management training, so the tactics in the evaluation strategy must be easily updated, and an expensive sales tracking system is not necessarily easy to update.
What are your expectations of a WLP evaluation strategy and resulting system?	Does the strategy meet management expectations? For example, the strategy may need to change, or education and communication of the strategy may be necessary to gain commitment.
Would you use information gathered in a WLP evaluation system? If so, how?	If management is not planning to use the information, who is, and why isn't management planning to use it?

and to what extent. When identifying the scope, you should be able to define:

1. what you expect to accomplish by implementing evaluation tools and methods
2. the amount of time, effort, and resources you will put into evaluation
3. the level of detail, or to what extent, or to what intensity you will evaluate
4. what limitations or parameters you will place on your evaluation efforts.

Table 1.6 lists examples of each of these factors.

Defining the scope of the evaluation strategy will help manage the "scope creep" that frequently happens when any project is implemented. *Scope creep* means that the original focus of the project expands to include other things, and it can result in the project taking longer to complete and requiring additional resources.

For example, you planned to do Level 2 (Learning), Level 3 (Behavior/Transfer), and Level 4 (Results) evaluation for a sales training program. But when you began to collect the data, you determined that the sales goals had changed between the time the baseline informa-

tion was collected and the postcourse measurement. It may take you a great deal of time and other resources to compile the data necessary to evaluate the new goals, only to be questioned by senior management anyway. Defining early on what information you need to obtain for the evaluation strategy will offset the panic and concern that arise as issues emerge during implementation.

Although defining the scope will not solve all scope creep issues, it will define what you expect to gain from the evaluation, what you see as your limitations, and to what extent you will use resources to resolve other issues. Table 1.7 lists various scope creep issues that can arise in implementing evaluation tools and how to modify the evaluation strategy to get to the information you need—without making evaluation the only thing the WLP department does.

Scope creep is most likely to happen when you are designing an evaluation strategy for a specific project or request, such as development of management training courseware or training for technology systems, new processes, or sales. An evaluation strategy scope can face tremendous issues if the project itself changes. You can manage the scope of the evaluation strategy by assessing the request using the following questions:

Table 1.6: Factors in Determining the Scope of the Strategy

Scope Factor	Example
Strategy accomplishments	Decision-making information for process improvements Customer satisfaction information WLP professional "trainer" performance data Design improvement information E-learning pilot information for further planning and decisions
Strategy time, effort, resources	No evaluation study will be engaged in for longer than 30 days Budget for evaluation efforts is $100,000 Two full-time-equivalent staff members will be assigned to evaluation efforts, and one will be a full-time administrative resource for reporting, computer support, and so forth
Strategy detail, extent, intensity	Level 4 (Results) will only use ballpark financial information Level 3 (Behavior/Transfer) data gathering will be at a high level, and no observations will be used Level 2 (Learning) testing information will not be used for hiring or performance information and will not be shared with managers
Strategy limitations, parameters	No field time will be used for evaluation No managers will be asked to participate in evaluation results Sales leads will only complete a form (that will take no longer than 15 minutes) one time per year Multirater 360 feedback information will only be sent to one outside individual per employee

Table 1.7: Resolving Scope Creep

Scope Creep Issue	Scope Creep Resolution
It is important to measure design against best practices. However, competencies do not exist, nor do designer performance standards.	Provide an instrument as a guide for designers to self-evaluate an intervention's design against industry best practices and identify areas for improvement.
Administration's registration system does not collect the type of demographic information that would be of value.	Determine what data it is necessary to collect to compare trends and provide evaluation information, but limit to essential details to promote confidentiality in evaluation responses.
Although there is a general feeling that having a Level 1 (Reaction) sheet is an important political statement to the participants in WLP products and services, it is agreed that Level 3 (Behavior/Transfer) data would be of much greater value.	Phase the evaluation strategy to begin development with a Level 3 component and follow it with other levels and evaluation tools as needed.
Testing is seen as a critical component to ensure workforce competence.	Establish test criteria and build tools that will evaluate the tests and report performance results.
Although there is a desire to have tools for all four evaluation levels, it is not practical to evaluate every course against all four levels.	Create a set of criteria that will determine which courses are evaluated at what levels.
Much of today's instruction is outsourced, and consequently the quality varies. There is a desire to set instructional standards.	Determine an evaluation system for instructor performance that promotes customer satisfaction, learning, and transfer back to the job.

- Will the evaluation method provide information that will improve a function, process, or structure? How does this align with the original request?
- Is the component of the evaluation strategy assessing how a structural problem was fixed (such as competencies) or providing additional information to address other problems (organizational needs) and how to remedy those problems?
- Is the issue a "nice to have" or a "have to have" in order for the performance solution to be effective?
- Will the resolution to the issue create a sounder structure for the product or service?
- Does the issue point to use of an assessment or evaluation criterion that will help WLP professionals improve or streamline their work practices?
- Does resolution of the issue ensure that quality of a product or service delivered by WLP will increase customer satisfaction?
- Will the results of implementing additional methods or tools (not currently provided by the evaluation strategy) provide information that can improve customer satisfaction?
- Will changes to the evaluation strategy provide information that promotes sound decision making and elevates the leadership position of WLP?

Structuring the Evaluation Strategy

Once you have defined the focus, business linkages, and scope of the evaluation strategy, you will be able to define the evaluation methods and goals that will deliver the results. Worksheets 1.1 and 1.2 should have jump-started this discussion, and as you defined the focus, business linkages, and scope, the structure should have become much clearer. The structure of the evaluation strategy includes the evaluation methods you chose in an earlier step. In addition, the structure involves

- timing (how often, when)
- media (e.g., Web-based, paper-based)
- participants in the evaluation
- data analysis methods

- key quality indicators (e.g., competitive advantage, best in class, improvement against baseline).

The structure may also provide the criteria for or prototypes of the tools to be used (such as client surveys, focus group questions, or test questions), although often the tools are not developed until the required parties have committed to the evaluation strategy.

Identifying Expected Results

You should identify expected results to validate the structure and scope of the evaluation strategy. Examples of results that are commonly identified in evaluation strategies include

- identification of opportunities for improvement to WLP practices and processes
- performance management information
- best-in-class comparison
- identification of customer value
- determination of level of customer satisfaction
- financial results
- job impact

- opportunities for knowledge growth and management
- identification of solutions that will close the performance gap
- assessment of current situation against standard
- identification of new needs
- alignment with business objectives
- progress toward goals.

Once you have identified the expected results, you should review them against the focus, scope, and structure to ensure that all are in alignment. Using table 1.8 as an example, identify the desired results from your evaluation strategy, and compare them to the scope. To ensure that they are aligned at this point, ask yourself the following questions:

- Will the scope as currently defined ensure that the evaluation will meet its desired results?
- How could the scope be better defined to ensure that the strategy's desired results will be met?
- Is the scope concise, or does it allow for multiple interpretations?

Table 1.8: Evaluation Strategy Desired Results

Desired Result	Scope	Focus	Structure
Evaluation of instructors to ensure that programs are consistent, outcomes are predictable, and instructional standards are met	To provide instructors with performance information and to determine which instructors will be used as key resources globally	The customers are participants in the program and in the organization's management There needs to be a balance between on-the-job results and customer satisfaction, as well as respect for instructor ability	Reaction sheet with instructor evaluation items Peer assessment that provides input on perceived strengths and weaknesses SME review that provides input on instructor knowledge and ability to discuss subject with degree of knowledge and skill On-the-job impact assessment to provide information on how instructor's participants were able to translate class information to the job
Improvement of overall design process for courseware to ensure effectiveness and efficiency in all media	To improve the current design process by identifying opportunities to change or modify it or provide tools to designers to expedite or improve design in all media	The customer's input on how user-friendly the design was in enabling them to understand content and use job-related tools outside of the classroom Understand how other organizations use processes and tools to ensure that the design of courseware across media provides business results	Use a structured evaluation during the pilot and on several random occasions when courseware is in use to specify design flaws and strengths Analyze design against specific design standards to ascertain opportunities for improvement Review best-in-class processes and tools and determine how they might be integrated into own WLP environment

Once you are comfortable with the strategy's desired results and scope, compare them to the focus using these questions:

- Does the focus provide multiple viewpoints?
- Is the focus balanced?
- If the focus of the evaluation strategy is acted on, will it provide results that will be accepted by all parties?

If you are satisfied with the results, scope, and focus, then compare the three to the structure of the evaluation strategy to ensure complete alignment:

- Does the structure provide information from all perspectives?
- Will the information provided by the structure meet the desired result objectives?
- Does the structure respect the scope of the project, or is it "out of scope"?

Identifying Resource Requirements

Once you have defined the methods and structure of the evaluation strategy, it is time to determine the human, financial, equipment, and other resources you will need to implement it. There are always cost and time associated with gathering, analyzing, and reporting evaluation results. Resource definition is the Achilles' heel of evaluation: Not specifying required resources can lead to unrealistic expectations, but if all costs are known, the value of evaluation might be questioned. This is why identifying what an evaluation strategy will accomplish and how it will be structured early in the strategy is so important. Defining the benefits before the costs is always a sound business strategy. Table 1.9 lists potential resource requirements to consider.

Table 1.9: Potential Resource Requirements for Evaluations

Type of Resource	Purpose of Resource
Human resources	Project lead or manager for the evaluation program itself. This may be the individual who owns the programs, department, or component. This individual is responsible for identifying the components to be measured.
	Evaluator. It is suggested that this person not be the individual responsible for the interventions being measured, which may bias results. This person is responsible for tool design or modification, implementation, analysis, reporting, and recommendations.
	Stakeholders. They will receive the final report and determine what actions will be undertaken.
System requirements	Systems must be in place to collect, analyze, and report the information. There may be a need for several systems such as a survey writer and reporter, a data spreadsheet tool (such as Excel), and a database management tool.
Technology resource requirements	New technology may be used for the data collection or reporting, such as a Web page or a chat room. Technology resources other than actual equipment or software are identified here.
Budget requirements	The budget requirements for the evaluation should be specified or estimated. A typical evaluation project from design to implementation costs between $25,000 and $50,000 depending on its complexity. A project is defined as a specific component of an evaluation strategy, such as benchmarking or measuring Level 3 results of a learning solution.
Capital expense requirements	If any capital expense requirements are foreseen (e.g., new computers), they should be identified.
Interface or other process owner requirements	Other process or interface owners and their time requirements need to be identified. Other process owners typically include managers of participants, participants in the intervention, instructors, financial analysts, and accountants.

Adapted with permission from Barksdale, Susan B., and Lund, Teri B. *What Evaluation Approach Provides the Biggest Payoff? Team and Organization Sourcebook.* Edited by Mel Silberman. New York: McGraw-Hill, 2001.

Integrating With Other Processes

Depending on the evaluation strategy's scope and expected results, the strategy may need to be linked with one or more WLP processes. Some of the most typical WLP and human resource processes that an evaluation strategy must link with are

- performance management
- certification
- quality management
- customer service delivery
- workplace learning delivery strategies
- staffing and succession planning
- six sigma.

Worksheet 1.4 will assist you in ensuring that the processes that need to integrate with the components of the evaluation strategy are identified and planned for. Remember, column 1 is for recording Level 1 (Reaction) or Level 2 (Testing) or another method discussed earlier in this chapter. Processes that need to be integrated are entered in the middle column, and the last column is for listing actions to take.

Identifying Reporting Requirements

Reporting requirements refer to the what, why, whom, how, and when of communicating the elements of the evaluation strategy. The evaluation strategy should identify whether Access, Excel, or other software packages will be used or whether a software package will

---

Worksheet 1.4: Process Integration Worksheet

Evaluation Methods	Processes to Be Integrated	Action Steps for Integration
Level 2 testing	Licensure requirements and contracting through human resources	Ensure that testing meets contract stipulations. Ensure that tests are legally defensible. Build a mechanism in the Level 2 testing process for grievances and accommodations for special needs.

Table 1.10: Reporting Requirement Criteria

Reporting Requirement	Definition	Criterion
What	The information that will be reported—for example, demographics of those involved in the evaluation of a workplace learning intervention	What information will be available What information will be standard (e.g., report date) What information can be accessed ad hoc
Why	The importance of the information that will be reported and how it will be used—for example, how the statistics for test questions will be used to determine test reliability and accuracy	Requirements for why the information is used Identification of any supporting documentation or directions that need to be made available to ensure that information can be used as needed
Who	The distribution of the reports: who will receive them and what information will be provided—for example, managers will receive a report with test scores for a Web-based class test	Identification of who gets what information Definition of security provisions if necessary for different levels of information by individual type
How	How the reports will be generated—for example, a report may be provided on the Web, on paper, or through individual email	The medium via which a report will be generated How access to the report will be provided Definition of security provisions, if necessary
When	The timing of the reports—for example, a report of participant reaction surveys will be generated seven days after a customer class is completed	Timing of the report Number of times the report will be offered Whether timing or offering differs by population (e.g., managers receive a copy before participants) Whether raw data will be available earlier and how

need to be developed, for example, to track Level 1 (Reaction) survey results. The reporting requirement criteria are explained in table 1.10.

Documenting the Strategy

Gaining commitment to an evaluation strategy is much easier when it appears organized and thorough. Documenting the strategy in a way that presents the thought and preparation that went into it using the outline in tool 1.1 will help you prepare an organized and thoughtful report for management that supports your strategy. As you proceed through the evaluation process, you will be very happy you have taken time to create this document.

Determining an Evaluation Strategy for an Intervention

Obviously, an evaluation strategy for a specific intervention is less comprehensive and much less difficult to execute than an organizational evaluation strategy. Table 1.11 illustrates how you can customize the contents of this chapter to create an evaluation strategy for a specific intervention (e.g., an EPSS or a Web-based training class). The time it takes to design an evaluation strategy for a specific intervention typically is one to five person-days, depending on the complexity of the intervention. This compares with approximately three to six months for an organizational strategy and 15 to 30 person-days for a departmental strategy, also depending on the complexity of the strategy.

Tool 1.1: Evaluation Strategy Contents

Purpose Definition

- primary business needs the evaluation will fill (no more than five)
- ways the evaluation strategy will support these needs (technologies, process, tools)
- primary focus of the evaluation strategy
- core competencies the evaluation strategy supports for the organization as a whole
- goals of the evaluation strategy
- organization's evaluation philosophy and its importance to its final deliverables
- purpose and expected results

Measurement Approaches

- the key metrics for the organization that will be gathered and reported through the evaluation system, including knowledge gain, customer satisfaction, ROI for the customer, and so forth
- the measures that will determine the value of the evaluation system itself, including use of data, number of process improvements identified as a result of the data, and so forth

Evaluation Structure and Scope Definition

- What the evaluation system will include, including the products, services, and deliverables that will be considered part of the evaluation system. How will the organization determine what program to evaluate at which of Kirkpatrick's four levels? At what frequency will each level be used? What standards will be used at each level?
- What elements will be included in each level?
- Who will make the decision about the components that will be included in the evaluation strategy (e.g., benchmarking, Levels 1 through 4)?
- What activities, technologies, or processes will be part of the evaluation strategy?
- Who are the customers of the evaluation strategy?

Integration With Other Processes

- the processes that will be included in the evaluation strategy data gathering and reporting
- how the processes will be integrated
- the methods and processes used to gather data for the strategy
- the information that will be captured in each process (Level 1 survey vs. Level 2 test)
- the analysis and reporting requirements for the process

Roles and Responsibilities

- Who is responsible for what components?
- Who are the key players?
- Who are the stakeholders?
- What are the roles (evaluation owner, project leader, data provider, partner, user, customer, consultant)?
- What are the responsibilities and accountabilities for each role?
- Who owns the data?
- What data are accessible, and by whom?
- Do different levels of evaluation have different owners?

Evaluation Tools

- a clear definition of what is and what is not included in the evaluation strategy
- prototypes, process flows, and design requirements for each of the levels and functions that will be supported by the evaluation strategy (such as instructor evaluation)

Reporting Requirements

- identification of each report, its contents, and distribution
- the data available through reporting, how the data is collected, the data source, and any potential data bias
- collection and reporting of quantitative versus qualitative data (comments)
- system requirements for reporting (e.g., ad hoc)
- data requirements for reporting
- distribution requirements

Resource Requirements

- human resource requirements
- system resource requirements
- technology resource requirements
- budget requirements
- capital expense requirements
- other requirements

Maintenance Plan (chapter 13)

- the owner of the maintenance plan
- frequency of review for maintenance
- events that will trigger maintenance
- how maintenance will be budgeted and managed

Communication Plan (chapter 3)

- the owner of communication of the evaluation strategy
- the methods for communicating the strategy
- the audiences for communication
- ongoing communication needs or communication points

Glossary and References

- evaluation terms used in strategy
- selected evaluation references

Adapted with permission from Barksdale, Susan B., and Lund, Teri B. *What Evaluation Approach Provides the Biggest Payoff? Team and Organization Sourcebook.* Edited by Mel Silberman. New York: McGraw-Hill, 2001.

Table 1.11: Contents of an Evaluation Strategy for an Intervention

Intevention Evaluation Strategy Step	Contents
Focus of evaluation strategy	What is important to evaluate regarding the intervention? Who are the customers of the intervention, and what are the specific needs of the customers regarding evaluation? What is the "balance" necessary for the intervention? What information is critical to track regarding the results of the intervention?
Business linkage	What are the business objectives this intervention supports? What should be evaluated to ensure the business objectives are supported as desired or needed?
Scope	What should be part of the evaluation strategy? What should not be part of the evaluation strategy?
Structure and method selection	What methods (e.g., reaction, testing) will the evaluation strategy include, and how will the methods be structured (e.g., timing, media approach)?
Expected results	What information will the evaluation strategy provide, and how will that information be used?
Resource requirements	What resources (e.g., financial, human, system, graphic design) will be needed?
Process integration	Is any integration with other processes needed?
Reporting requirements	What are the reporting requirements for the evaluation of the intervention?
Project management linkage	How will the evaluation strategy components be integrated into the design, development, and implementation of the intervention itself or its project plan?

Chapter Summary

This chapter introduced and discussed the first step of the evaluation process: determining the evaluation strategy. The need for and purpose of an evaluation strategy were presented, along with the benefits of such a strategy. Case examples describing how three companies developed evaluation strategies were provided to help illustrate this step. The importance of identifying the focus, business linkages, structure, expected results, and required resources for an evaluation strategy was discussed and developed, as was the need to link the evaluation strategy to other key WLP processes. How to report the evaluation results and how to document the strategy were addressed. Finally, determining an evaluation strategy for a specific intervention was discussed.

Discussion Questions

The following questions are provided to help you discuss what you have learned in this chapter:

- Why is an evaluation strategy for WLP needed in your or your customer's organization? What purpose will it serve?

_____

_____

- What are two benefits to the organization of developing an evaluation strategy?

  _____

  _____

- What two methods for gathering data would be needed for an evaluation strategy for your or your customer's organization?

  _____

  _____

- Why is it important for an evaluation strategy to be focused?

  _____

  _____

- Why is it critical to link an evaluation strategy to business goals?

  _____

  _____

- Why is it important to be clear about the scope and structure of an evaluation strategy?

  _____

  _____

- Why should the expected results of the evaluation strategy be identified?

  _____

  _____

- What is the Achilles' heel of an evaluation strategy, and why?

  _____

  _____

- What are two processes that an evaluation strategy might need to be integrated with?

  _____

  _____

- Why is identifying the reporting requirements for the evaluation strategy important?

  _____

  _____

- What purpose does documenting the evaluation strategy serve?

  _____

  _____

- What is the main difference between an evaluation strategy for an intervention versus an organizational evaluation strategy?

  _____

  _____

References

Barksdale, Susan B., and Lund, Teri B. *What Evaluation Approach Provides the Biggest Payoff? Team and Organization Sourcebook*. Edited by Mel Silberman. New York. McGraw-Hill, 2001.

Kaplan, Robert, and Norton, David. *The Balanced Scorecard*. Boston: Harvard Business Press, 1996.

Kirkpatrick, Donald L. *Evaluating Training Programs*. San Francisco: Berrett-Koehler Publishers, 1994.

Establishing Measures

When you embark on an organizational evaluation strategy, one of the biggest challenges is determining what results to measure and how to measure them. Establishing the measures is often what stops evaluation plans in their tracks. A *measure* is a standard used to assess the results of a performance intervention. This chapter provides a simple process for determining what to measure along with tools and practices that can assist you in establishing measures.

Whether as part of an organizational evaluation strategy or for an individual intervention or WLP product or service, measuring results is important to the success of WLP products and services. This chapter addresses the following:

- case examples illustrating how to establish measures

- validating the business drivers and performance needs

- determining the measurement approach

- applying measurement criteria to determine issues and concerns

- selecting the intensity of the measurement

- aligning the measures with the strategy or intervention objectives

- reviewing the evaluation strategy and measures.

It is essential to the evaluation that you select measures *before* designing and developing the intervention. Although it is possible to develop and implement evaluation postdesign, a key benefit is lost by doing so. If you build evaluation as early as possible into the intervention development process, you will discover additional information that is important to both the evaluation and the intervention itself. The following three case examples illustrate the importance of using the measures to validate the business need, structure the design and development of the intervention, and determine the structure of the measurement process.

Case Examples

Case Example 1

Quality Valve Manufacturers sought to evaluate a new WLP development model it was using. The purpose of the model was to decrease design time while confirming the correlation of the results to the performance needs. The company wanted to demonstrate that the model had improved WLP's approach to design and that business needs and performance goals were met more quickly.

Unfortunately, the need for the evaluation was identified after the model was developed. Although the company realized a return-on-investment (ROI) for the performance model and improved the design as well as performance, two flaws were uncovered through the evaluation process:

1. Performance measures changed after the intervention was in place. Thus, although the data was normalized, part of the performance improvement measurement was lost because the data no longer existed.
2. As the process of identifying measures began, a large design flaw emerged. Had evaluation been part of the needs assessment or early design, the flaw would have been detected before the intervention was implemented. As a result, a large revision was warranted.

The company quickly saw the importance of establishing measures and doing evaluation, but it also learned that the earlier this is done, the better.

Case Example 2

Company AOK's primary product is the delivery of "canned" instructional programs that are offered by external resources who have the technical ability to deliver the material. AOK contracts with these resources for instructional time either in the classroom or through Web-facilitated training. In the past AOK had participants complete a simple reaction sheet and used the feedback from that to provide performance feedback to instructors. However, the company had grown significantly, as had its competition. It was now a global company that needed to provide consistent, quality WLP products to maintain its competitive advantage.

As a result, AOK's key evaluation strategy was to revamp the instructor evaluation methods. To establish measures and methods to evaluate instructors, AOK first determined what the business goals for the instructors were, then decided that it needed an approach that used best practice standards from outside sources to develop a three-dimension instructor evaluation that included peer assessment, subject matter expert (SME) evaluation, and a more intensive participant feedback process.

AOK found that this evaluation strategy and measurement mix provided the feedback needed to measure the performance of its instructors and to ensure that its products met or exceeded customer expectations.

Case Example 3

Testing had always played a key role in the evaluation strategy of High Performance Engineering Company. However, it found that the results back on the job did not necessarily match the test results. Consequently, it determined that the measures used to determine the level of learning that occurred needed to consider skill development, and not just acquisition of knowledge. Using a form of Bloom's taxonomy (Bloom, 1956) to identify the level of skill development that should be measured, an evaluation approach for Kirkpatrick's Level 2 (Learning) was structured (Kirkpatrick, 1994). This approach included testing, observations, and laboratory assessment.

Validating Business Drivers

Whether you establish measures for a strategy or specific intervention, the most important step is to validate the business drivers (Barksdale and Lund, 1998). *Business drivers* are the internal and external forces that direct an organization's strategy, goals, business needs, and performance needs. Validation involves identifying the business drivers, determining whether they still exist, and ascertaining that they can be affected by the intervention. Business drivers are generated both externally and internally. External business drivers are outside of an organization's control and typically include the following:

- *economic drivers:* upturns or downturns in the economy, embargoes or trade restrictions, other economically driven situations

- *human resource drivers:* shortages of resources or of certain skills, union demands or contracts, employee needs to balance family and work relationships

- *government drivers:* regulation or deregulation that forces changes in competition or the environment as a whole

- *public perception drivers:* the public's view of the organization, sometimes influenced by press coverage of an event or situation outside the organization's control

- *market or customer drivers:* changes in customer demographics, definition, and needs that place demands on products or change product design; increased competition or other changes in how the organization views the marketplace in which it competes.

Internal business drivers are generated by internal decisions. Sometimes an internal business driver is a response to an external business driver. There typically is a stakeholder inside the organization for this type of driver, an important consideration in creating a performance improvement strategy. Internal drivers include the following:

- *technology drivers:* new innovations and technology that create opportunities or needs for changes in information keeping and processing

- *change in system, process, or key policy drivers:* changes in work processes, systems, or key policies that change employee skill or behavior requirements

- *shareholder or financial drivers:* responses to investor or bank demands for higher profits or lower costs reflected on the balance sheet

- *new product generation drivers:* responses to market or customer changes that result in new product or service generation or revision to meet demand or need.

Responses to the Business Driver

An organization formulates business objectives and strategies to respond to the business driver. For example, if the business driver is increased competition, a response may be to cut costs in other parts of the organization to reduce prices to the customer and undercut the competition.

The performance need defines what employees need to achieve to support the business driver and corresponding business response. For example, if increasing market share is an identified business driver, the business response is to sell more products to a customer within the product family. The performance need identified is increased product knowledge and recognition of which products within the product family complement each other and are potential prospects for a particular customer base.

Performance needs usually drive a training program or performance intervention. The same performance needs define the value of the intervention to the organization and justify the organization's investment in it. It must be kept in mind that not all causes of performance problems indicate a need for or can be solved by training. The problem is often multifaceted, and so is the solution. It is therefore important to determine what training can actually contribute to the performance results, especially before investing funds in design and development.

Linking with Measures

Identifying business drivers is fundamental to the determination of evaluation measures, regardless whether the evaluation method will be comparison to best practices, Level 3 (Behavior/Transfer) evaluation, or an internal audit for design practices. Once you identify the business driver, the criteria for what must be included in the measurement will follow, as demonstrated in table 2.1.

Table 2.1: Applying Business Driver Identification (Increased Reliance on Technology) to Performance Need and Evaluation Method

Business Driver	Performance Need	Evaluation Method
Increased reliance on technology	Increase employees' comfort with and ability to use technology in the workplace	Level 1 (Reaction): participant perception survey
	Increase employees' knowledge and use of technology postintervention	Level 2 (Learning): application demonstration through laboratory assessments and structured observations
	Increase employees' ability to use technology back on the job	Level 3 (Behavior/Transfer): participant performance comparison by job observation and performance diary
	Increase business results for technology	Level 4 (Results): pre-post comparison of business indicators such as decreased time to proficiency and call time for customer inquiries; perception among competitors as technologically advanced company
	Align company with best practices in technology use or application	Best practice identification: comparison to a study on best practices done before intervention
	Increase employees' ability to use practices identified as technology transfer best practices	Practice audit: review (postintervention) of whether employees are transferring technology best practices back to the job

The measures that will be most meaningful to your organization must be based on the business drivers. An example of how to link driver to measures is provided in table 2.2. It shows how a business driver, either external or internal, can be linked to a performance need and measure. Note that if the driver is external, there are more barriers to meeting the performance need, since external drivers are typically more volatile. By linking the performance need to a business driver (if affected parties agree on the linkage), you can select an adequate measure.

For example, if the business driver is government regulation, then the performance need is to ensure that employees' performance meets the regulation requirements. The WLP practice must support people in developing, sustaining, and using the desired performance to meet the regulation requirements, and the measures must ensure that the organization's personnel perform to regulation and that no penalties or exceptions will be identified by regulators.

You may need to do more probing to identify the relationship between performance needs and the WLP intervention's objectives. Worksheet 2.1 can facilitate discussion about what the needs are and what measures are required. Go through the questions listed in part 1 and identify the questions and measurement methods that are most closely related to the evaluation (strategy or intervention) need that has been

Table 2.2: Linking Business Drivers and Performance Needs to Measures

Business Driver	Performance Need	Measure
Competition (external)	Increase presence in market; key competitors are offering products in new marketplaces on an ongoing basis	Market share for products sold and supported by licensed franchises (%)
Human resource (internal)	Enable employees and licensed employees to understand, sell, and support new product lines	Increase in product knowledge (%)

identified. Then move on to part 2 and align the measures in the individual, business, or financial categories. Finally, use the questions in part 3 to analyze the measures.

By identifying measures in the three categories identified in part 2 of worksheet 2.1 (individual, business, and financial), you have defined the measurement approach. If you identified many more critical measures in the individual category than in the other two, then the measurement approach should be targeted more to customer satisfaction, learning, and on-the-job transfer, or performance improvement and career development. Likewise, if you identified more critical measures in the business category, you should assess customer satisfaction but focus on business standardization, results, and on-the-job business impact. Finally, if most critical measures were in the financial category, the focus should be on results, standardization, cost comparison, and best practices.

Typically, you will have identified several measures at this point. Using three to five sound measures is a realistic goal. If you use more than five measures (whether at the strategy or intervention level), the evaluation will most likely become cumbersome and time consuming, and the results of your evaluation will not be significantly greater because of the added work. If you use fewer than three measures, you may find it difficult to analyze conflicting data gathered during the evaluation and to produce usable conclusions and recommendations.

You can judge each measure for its quality by asking six questions:

1. Does the measure reflect business objectives?

2. Is the measure valued by top management?

3. Can the measure be computed for specific employees?

4. Is the measurement data available on a timely basis?

5. Can enough data be collected for reliable measurement?

6. Is the measure free from known bias? That is, is it free from contamination by preconceived ideas, faulty assumptions, or evaluator prejudice?

Each yes answer represents one point. A high-quality measure will receive a 6; a measure that receives a rating of less than 4 should be reconsidered and potentially eliminated.

Determining the Measurement Approach

Once you have identified the business drivers and performance needs and their related measures, your next task is to determine the measurement approach. *Measurement approach* refers to how you will perform the measurement, like administer a test or observe on-the-job performance or calculate ROI. For WLP practices, the measurement approach is centered most often on what level of Kirkpatrick's evaluation model you will follow, but other models may be used as well. For example, your evaluation method may be a Level 1 reaction sheet, and the measurement approach would define what would be included on the sheet (e.g., instructor ability, relevance of material, quality of content), which is what will be measured. Table 2.3 identifies the various types of measurement approaches by category and briefly describes each. Selecting the approach can be confusing—and more evaluation is not necessarily better. Instead, it is important for you to identify what information is truly valuable in determining if the WLP intervention met its expected results.

Individual Measurement Approaches

An early WLP method—Bloom's taxonomy—can assist in determining the measurement approach

Worksheet 2.1: Defining Measures Linked to Business Needs

Part 1: Data-Gathering Questions

What knowledge increase do you expect to see from participants (e.g., product knowledge, customer knowledge, technical knowledge)?

_____

_____

What on-the-job evidence would you look for as a result of this knowledge increase (e.g., lower product costs, manufacturing or marketing relationships improved, decreased time to proficiency)?

_____

_____

What skill increase do you expect to see from participants (e.g., communication skills, presentation skills, computer skills)?

_____

_____

What on-the-job evidence would you look for as a result of this skill increase (e.g., ability to explain product features and benefits, ability to plan meetings, ability to use Excel to enter budget data)?

_____

_____

What business impact would you expect overall from implementation of the strategy or intervention (e.g., productivity increase, overall decrease in costs, technology used where it had not been before)?

_____

_____

How would you know if this change had occurred—through what means (e.g., organizational reports, manager feedback, informal reports of improved employee morale)?

_____

_____

Do you currently measure the expected change at the employee level, and, if so, through what vehicle (e.g., performance evaluations, organizational reports, observation)?

_____

_____

How would you know if the change had not occurred? What would be the evidence (e.g., no impact or change, continued decrease in morale, loss of market share)?

_____

_____

For a specific intervention only: What instigated the request for the intervention? What is the primary driving business force creating this need (e.g., loss of market share, absenteeism, increase in tardiness or grievances, new product line)?

_____

_____

(continued next page)

Worksheet 2.1: Defining Measures Linked to Business Needs *(continued)*

Part 1: Data-Gathering Questions *(continued)*

Have performance criteria to support the strategy or intervention been defined (e.g., by employee percent of error reduction, percent of sales increase, number of policies input)?

_____

_____

What (if any) factors outside of the strategy or intervention might influence the results realized from the products or services delivered (e.g., disgruntlement over pay, lack of management support for the change, lack of on-the-job measurement of change, new computer system not available after training)?

_____

_____

Can the existing performance be measured today to create a baseline? If so, how (e.g., organizational reports, creation of a form for measurement, management evaluation)?

_____

_____

Part 2: Identifying Measures

Focus of Measure	Specific Measures You Need	Reporting Methods for Each Measure
Individual measures: measures that are related to an individual's knowledge or skill. These measures must be able to be tracked at the employee level. An example of this measure is no. of sales closed by an employee.	(List answers from questions 1, 2, 3, 4, and 7)	
Business measures: measures that are specific to the type of business and measure the impact on the business (may not be reported at an employee level). Examples are productivity increase, product sales, and compliance with regulations.	(List answers from questions 2, 4, 5, 6, 8, 9, 10, 11, and 12)	
Financial measures: measures that are directly related to the bottom line or spreadsheet (most likely not reported at an employee level).	(List answers from questions 2, 5, 6, 10, 11, and 12)	
Other measures that do not fit in the above categories:		

Part 3: Analyses of Part 2

Is the measure related to the strategy or intervention understandable to the instructors and participants? Will they understand how the content is linked to the business measure? If the measure is not widely understood, it is probably a poor choice to use in Level 1 tools.

_____

_____

Is there linkage between measures, and, if so, how? An individual measure, if met, would most likely influence other measures. For example, number of employee sales closed most likely would increase overall product sales and increase revenue for the company. Measures with linkages to all three categories typically are the most critical to the business and the most important to measure.

_____

_____

Are there any contrary measures—measures that would identify if the strategy or intervention did not have an impact? For example, if errors were increasing and the intervention does not work, errors will continue to rise.

_____

_____

Are there any reports that are used for all categories (e.g., a sales report)? Such reports are usually a good resource for measures of the impact of the strategy or intervention and baseline data.

_____

_____

What measures are most closely linked to the content of the strategy or intervention?

_____

_____

Table 2.3: Types of Measurement Approaches

Evaluation Method	Measurement Approach	Description of Approach
Level 1 (Reaction)	Participant surveys	These can be either long form or short form and provide general information on the participant's or user's perception of the WLP intervention.
	Focus groups	Often used in conjunction with surveys, the focus group answers more detailed questions to provide specific information on participants' or users' reactions to the content, instruction, media, or other element of the WLP intervention.
	Interviews	This very specific approach usually focuses on a small sample of carefully chosen users or participants to solicit specific concerns, issues, or detailed feedback.

(continued next page)

Table 2.3: Types of Measurement Approaches *(continued)*

Evaluation Method	Measurement Approach	Description of Approach
Level 2 (Learning)	Tests	Tests are a series of questions or items used to measure the skill or knowledge acquired through the WLP intervention.
	Structured observations	Observations are structured with step-by-step checklists to determine if the participant or user is using the desired knowledge or skill during the intervention or training.
	Laboratory assessments	These assess the use of information or equipment in a specified environment to create or resolve a defined outcome.
	Self-efficacy assessments	These assessments measure the increase (or decrease) in an individual's confidence level.
Level 3 (Behavior/Transfer)	Perception surveys	These include a set of questions designed to gain general information on the perception of transfer to the job by the user or participant of the WLP intervention.
	Performance indicators	Measures are compared with pre-established performance indicators (e.g., errors, sales, output) by individual. A baseline measurement for comparison is required in this method.
	Structured observations	Observations are structured with step-by-step checklists to determine if the participant or user is using the desired knowledge or skill back on the job.
	Performance diaries	This structured method gathers a participant's or user's self-reports of daily tasks and any barriers or additional performance information as needed.
	Coaching transfer evaluations	A "coach" or manager back on the job conducts a specific evaluation to determine the amount and type of transfer of the WLP intervention to the job.
	Expert evaluations	Evaluation by a SME assesses whether the user or participant has transferred the expertise back to the job.
	Impact analysis	The cause and effect of a WLP intervention back on the job is analyzed using probable leading or lagging indicators.
Level 4 (Results)	Individual performance metrics	Specific performance metrics (e.g., sales, telephone calls, errors) that should have been affected by the WLP intervention are tracked by individual. This type of evaluation requires a baseline.
	Organizational performance metrics	Specific performance metrics (e.g., scrap, product penetration, customer satisfaction) that should have been affected by the WLP intervention are tracked at the organization (or group) level. This type of evaluation requires a baseline.
	ROI models or other financial indicators	ROI models (e.g., break-even, months for payback) or other financial indicators (e.g., price earning ratio, accounts payable period) that should have been affected by the WLP intervention are tracked. This type of evaluation requires a baseline.

Evaluation Method	Measurement Approach	Description of Approach
Other	Performance audits	Organizational performance to plan or to a set of established standards are tracked.
	Best practice comparisons	A group's or individual's performance is measured against established best practice standards.
	Peer analysis	Peers use agreed-on criteria to evaluate each other's work.
	Expert review	Experts observe or review results to ensure credibility and accuracy.

when the focus is the individual, specifically when Kirkpatrick's Levels 2 through 4 are being considered. Table 2.4 describes the six cognitive levels that are part of Bloom's taxonomy and matches them with Kirkpatrick's levels 2 through 4 of evaluation.

Bloom's taxonomy can provide a focal point for evaluating the participant's purpose in using or attending the intervention. For example, a premise of Company XYZ's evaluation strategy is to ensure that its employees understand and can apply the policies and procedures for providing customer service and resolving customer problems. Regardless of department or customer problem, the employee should be able to use the customer service procedure to solve customer problems on his or her own. Consequently, Company XYZ's evaluation strategy should focus on Bloom's tax-

onomy domain of application and evaluate at Level 2 or 3 or some combination.

In another example, a specific intervention for Workplace Products Unlimited is to ensure that product managers are able to look at customer trends, product issues and complaints, and competition market strategies and devise new product strategies. The intervention's purpose is to help product managers work at Bloom's taxonomy domain of synthesis, and the evaluation level for this intervention must be at Level 3. Additional information about how to design methods for measurement approaches at Levels 2 through 4 is offered in chapters 5, 6, and 7.

WLP customer satisfaction information is best gathered using Kirkpatrick's Levels 1 and 3. The perception of customer satisfaction after an intervention

Table 2.4: Relationship of Bloom's Taxonomy to Kirkpatrick's Evaluation Levels 2 Through 4

Cognitive Level	Evaluation Level	Description
Evaluation	Level 3 or 4	This is the highest level of Bloom's taxonomy. Someone working at this level can assess the value of ideas and appropriateness or usefulness of an object, plan, or design. An individual at this level must be able to judge if another individual can operate or demonstrate the ability to work at all of the lower levels. Evaluation would need to occur at Level 3 or 4 to identify if an individual is working at this level of ability.
Synthesis	Level 3	This level requires the ability to use parts to assemble the whole. Given a set of data someone working at this level would create totally original material. Working at this level, one can integrate information and is working at an optimal level. For example, one is able to adapt to a changing environment and to think strategically, patterns are recognized and interpreted, themes are identified, and dynamic relationships of information are understood. An assessment of evaluation at Level 3 would be necessary to determine ability at this cognitive level.

(continued next page)

Table 2.4: Relationship of Bloom's Taxonomy to Kirkpatrick's Evaluation Levels 2 Through 4 *(continued)*

Cognitive Level	Evaluation Level	Description
Analysis	Level 2 or 3	The ability to break the whole into parts is evident at this level. Complex situations can be broken into component parts and then separated into groups to determine how the parts relate to and influence each other. Someone working at this level can be given extensive data (only some of which is relevant to the solution) and solve a problem by determining which data is important to the solution. This level of ability could be evaluated at Level 2 and 3.
Application	Level 2 or 3	At this level of application one uses what has been previously learned. One is able to identify what information, rules, or formulas to use when presented with a problem. In other words, information and rules can be applied to new situations to determine solutions or resolutions. This level of ability could be evaluated at Level 2 and 3.
Comprehension	Level 2	At this level the ability to translate information, apply designated rules, or recognize what is new material or new concepts is present. The comprehension level is more than simple rote memorization. For example, someone working at the knowledge level might be able to cite the features of a product or products. But someone working at the comprehension level would be able to describe those features in his or her own words. This level of ability can be evaluated with Level 2 instruments.
Knowledge	Level 2	At this level the ability to recall information or remember content is present. Examples of the type of knowledge that is included in this category are definitions, procedures, formulas, and directions. A person working at a knowledge level would be able to write the steps in a procedure. An individual working at this cognitive level can be evaluated with Level 2 instruments.

is usually captured by gathering information from the participants (and possibly their respective managers) or the person paying. The methods for this approach are further defined in chapters 4 and 6.

Business Measurement Approaches

There are two types of measurement approaches for the business category: those that apply to the business of the WLP customer and those that apply to the WLP business itself. In identifying which information is truly valuable to the business of the WLP customer, it may be helpful to ask questions such as the following: Are the business objectives met as a result of the strategy's products and services or a specific intervention? Are managers coaching their employees appropriately? Is retention increasing? Are customer complaints decreasing? Is the business more competitive? Are costs lowering per product? Are employees spending less time on

the phone answering customer questions, yet improving customer satisfaction? Measuring the responses to these questions commonly involves Levels 3 (Behavior/ Transfer) or 4 (Results) methods and others such as performance audits, expert reviews, cost comparison studies, and competitive or mystery shopping studies (in the latter, researchers pose as customers in a customer-driven organization and use a set of published standards to rate the performance of service or sales personnel). Methods for this type of approach are discussed in chapters 6, 7, and 8.

Identifying the most valuable information for evaluating the business of WLP may involve asking the following questions: Do the products and services meet the needs and standards of the customers whom WLP professionals serve? Are the practices of WLP efficient, standard, and cost-effective? Although all of the previously identified approaches and methods provide information that address these questions, peer analysis and expert review may be the most effective approaches to determine what needs changing. These methods are discussed in chapter 8.

Financial Measurement Approaches

Finally, approaches to measure a financial result may be required. The financial need may be expressed in two ways:

1. by some related financial indicator—for example, percentage of payroll spent on WLP practices, average collection period, asset turnover, or productivity of assets

2. by some type of cost comparison—for example, is less spent on sales training than the competition with greater results, or is more spent on sales training with fewer results?

These approaches naturally are more time consuming but still can be very valuable. The methods for these approaches are defined in chapters 7 and 8.

The primary evaluation methods used for WLP practices are Kirkpatrick's four levels of evaluation. Worksheet 2.2 provides additional decision criteria that will be integrated into the measurement approach for each evaluation method. The decision criteria are presented to provide food for thought about why you might want to use a measurement approach or an evaluation method you may have previously ruled out.

Applying Measurement Criteria

Even though you have defined the measurement approach, it is still important to understand where measurement issues and concerns lie. Each approach has its own barriers to collecting the desired data. Can you actually obtain competitor information? Will the participants in a Web-based class take the time to complete a reaction survey? Will users see value in completing a questionnaire that asks for information about how they use an electronic performance support system (EPSS) on the job? Recognizing potential problems early on and planning for them is more likely to ensure your success in implementing the evaluation strategy overall. The checklist provided in worksheet 2.3 is an example of how to begin identifying potential problems with the implementation of an evaluation approach.

You should identify and define these issues and concerns in the evaluation strategy or implementation project plan and explain steps to manage the issues. For example, no one is trained in evaluation. What steps (e.g., education, hiring an external expert) should be taken to address the risk and get to the desired evaluation results? Remember always to emphasize the benefit of evaluation first and then gain the commitment needed to overcome the barriers to it.

Selecting the Intensity of the Measurement

Once you have identified the approach for an evaluation strategy or intervention, the question is, How intense must the evaluation be? *Intensity* refers to the extent of effort or amount of information needed. Frequently, a Level 3 or 4 evaluation method is not used because it is seen as too labor or cost intensive. It need not be this way, depending on the situation. You may be able to gather valuable data with less effort. Or, if data is unavailable, using a less intensive measurement approach may still provide enough information to make a sound decision. Many factors make up the final decision, including time, resources, budget, data requirements, and type of decision that will be made from the data. The tiers of intensity are as follows:

- *Low intensity:* This intensity level is predominantly perception driven and does not attempt to quantify data or classify it to a specific degree. For example, a low-intensity evaluation at Level 1 would include a Likert scale of 5 that defines only the highest and lowest levels. The values are not clearly anchored to a meaning, and there is some interpretation done by whoever is completing the instrument.

- *Moderate intensity:* Data at this level of intensity is viewed statistically as having a qualitative value or a low level of quantitative value. The data is finite and measurable but is not in-depth and exhaustive.

- *High intensity:* Data at this level is in-depth and exhaustive. The data is often validated and tied to specific people, costs, or measures.

The level of intensity needs to match the value of the output for the organization. Are the results from a low-intensity evaluation going to meet the organization's need? Is a high-intensity effort worth it? Table 2.5 describes measurement approaches appropriate for

Worksheet 2.2: Defining Evaluation Needs
Using Kirkpatrick's Evaluation Levels

Evaluation Method	Decision Criteria for Measurement Approaches	Yes or No
Level 1 (Reaction)	Is it important to gather opinions regarding content usefulness, instructor ability, timing, and other factors in this intervention?	
	Is the course brand new? Should customer reaction be collected for at least a short period of time?	
	Is there some potential problem with the course that needs to be monitored (e.g., instructor, facility, delivery method)?	
Level 2 (Learning)	Is it critical that the individual learn the content in the course (e.g., safety requirements, government requirements, job performance, certification)?	
	Is it politically important to demonstrate that there has been knowledge acquisition or skill development as a result of the solution?	
	Is it important to determine how effective the intervention was (e.g., when a new delivery method is being used)?	
	Is it important to determine what has *not* been learned so another intervention can be given (e.g., coaching, other coursework)?	
	Is it important to capture objectives or content that most of the participants are either gaining or missing as a result of this course (e.g., effectiveness of particular content, need for follow-up module, effectiveness of a guest instructor)?	
Level 3 (Behavior/Transfer)	Was the launch of this intervention based on the business results it would provide?	
	Is it important to determine what in the work environment is a barrier to the transfer?	
	Is it important to determine what skills, knowledge, or behavior change has *not* occurred?	
	Is it of value to management to determine if what has been taught is being used?	
	Is it important to determine the degree of skill or knowledge transfer?	
Level 4 (Results)	Is this solution critical to business needs, and will the results be valued by management therefore as justifying the time and expense required by a Level 4 evaluation?	
	Is the cost of the delivery method or solution high?	
	Is it important to determine which skill or knowledge taught has the biggest payoff in results? Is this	
	program a pilot of a larger effort, and therefore financial results are required for implementation?	

Worksheet 2.3: Risk Assessment Checklist

Potential Problem	Might this problem affect the organization? (yes or no)	How high is the risk? (1 = low, 3 = high)
No one is trained in evaluation, or there is no evaluation expertise in the organization.		
Adequate resources (e.g., human, financial) are not available to undertake this evaluation.		
Management believes we do the best job possible and does not think evaluation will provide us with any better information. Management, for whatever reason, is not committed to this evaluation.		
The data we need is not believed to exist or is unavailable.		
Evaluation is thought to be too time consuming, and the process needed to get to the data confirms this.		
The participants or users will not have time, incentive, or motivation to provide us with the information needed.		
The business purpose and objectives are not in alignment or are misunderstood.		
The problem is outside WLP practice, and all the evaluation approach will do is point this out again.		
We already have implemented the intervention we planned to evaluate.		
We have an evaluation tool for this now, but it is not adequate.		
We have chosen several approaches for evaluation and are concerned that the scope of the strategy is too big.		
We need to gather competitive information but are concerned about how to do that ethically and legally.		

each of Kirkpatrick's evaluation levels and each level of intensity.

Readdressing case example 2 mentioned earlier in this chapter, Company AOK had used a low-intensity reaction survey for instructor evaluation that was adequate. But following changes in the organization and competition, AOK needed to implement a much more intense evaluation approach and methods. AOK needed a more diverse and complete level of information to provide feedback to the instructors and to make external staffing decisions globally. Consequently, AOK implemented a high-intensity evaluation program for instructor performance feedback.

Seven key factors are listed in worksheet 2.4. Rank each factor on a scale of 1 to 7 to indicate each factor's importance to you. If you rank the majority of factors 3 or less, you can most likely do a low-intensity evaluation. However, if you rank any factor with a 6 or 7, you

Table 2.5: Measurement Approach Intensity Characteristics

Evaluation Method	Low-Intensity Characteristics	Moderate-Intensity Characteristics	High-Intensity Characteristics
Level 1 (Reaction)	Undefined Likert scale (allows for interpretation) Open-ended questions Broad data not tied to specific planning, quality, and customer satisfaction objectives	Anchored survey statements (leaves little to no room for interpretation) Specific questions tied to content, delivery, or value Data tied to specific planning, quality, and customer satisfaction objectives	Interviews or focus groups with participants or managers postcourse Specific interview or questioning script Data tied to specific planning, quality, and customer satisfaction objectives
Level 2 (Learning)	Test using behavior-anchored statements (subjective) Unstructured observations Self-efficacy assessments that identify perceived learning change	Structured tests that have been evaluated for reliability and viability Structured observation checklist (completed by instructor, peer, other participant, or coach)	Structured tests that have been validated Structured observation checklist completed by objective expert
Level 3 (Behavior/Transfer)	Follow-up surveys with undefined Likert scale, open-ended questions that allow for interpretation	Anchored survey statements (leave little to no room for interpretation) Structured observation checklist (completed by manager or coach) Focus groups with structured scripts Interviews with structured scripts	Productivity or individual performance metrics (number of closed sales, call wait times, re-work statistics, return customers) Mystery shopping Structured observation checklist completed by objective expert
Level 4 (Results)	Follow-up surveys of approximate impact on business or financial indicators identified	Business or financial measures without separation of training or historic factors	Normalized business or financial measures Business and financial measures reported on an individual basis
Other	Published information and studies (e.g., a baseline study published for the WLP industry) used as the basis for the comparison data needed to assess the quality of your organization's WLP practices	Design standards from information collected during a study conducted by your own organization that can be used to create a set of evaluation instruments to assess the quality of WLP practices within your organization.	Have an external firm collect data from external sources and your organization using a set of best practices and then compare the data across organizations Provide your organization with the results, conclusions, and recommendations particular to your own organization

should review that category and determine how you might incorporate the significance of that factor in a low-intensity approach.

For example, Company AOK, when ranking the Intensity Decision Matrix, ranked "importance of data to organization," "decision impact of evaluation data," and "budget" with 6s and 7s. The other factors were ranked with a 3 or lower. Knowing that the budget for evaluation was limited, management felt that a low-intensity evaluation would garner information they could use in instructor performance management. To supplement a more intense reaction sheet, Company AOK also used SME evaluations and peer assessments of instructors randomly. Each instructor's performance was reviewed twice a year by a peer and SME.

If you rank the majority of factors with either a 4 or 5, then consider a moderate-intensity approach. In this case it is probably easier to incorporate any factors with a 6 or 7. If you rank the majority of factors with either a 6 or 7, then a high-intensity approach is necessary.

It is important to view your comments as well as the rankings, especially if the choice of intensity is

Worksheet 2.4: Intensity Decision Matrix

Factor for Consideration	Rank of Importance (7 = most important, 1 = least important)	Comments
Importance of data to the organization		
• The data is important to better understand issues, problems, and barriers.	_____	
• The data is important to prioritize other work.	_____	
• The data will support other studies.	_____	
• The organization does not have access to this data currently and needs it.	_____	
• The data is important for customer satisfaction.	_____	
Decision impact from evaluation data		
• The decisions made from the data will affect human resource performance, salaries, and career development.	_____	
• The decisions made from the data will influence short- and long-term decisions.	_____	
• The decisions from this data will have an impact on planning and resource allocation.	_____	
Participant time		
• It is important for participants to be included, and their time is worth the results.	_____	
• It is important to include participants, but this is a lower priority and their jobs fill their time.	_____	
Resource requirements		
• It is important to consider resource priorities and time availability.	_____	
• Amount of resources that can be made available for evaluation may be limited.	_____	
• Specific resource characteristics are needed (e.g., education level, type of job) to ensure that measurement data are correct.	_____	
Budget		
• Finances are limited.	_____	
• Dollars are available if the results are worthy.	_____	
Length of time between evaluation and results		
• It is important to have immediate results.	_____	
• The results are more important than how long it will take to get them.	_____	
• There is a tolerance for some delay between the intervention, the evaluation, and the results.	_____	
Data accessibility		
• The data is difficult to obtain.	_____	
• Normalization of data must take place.	_____	
• Data ownership is unclear.	_____	
• There are legal or ethical issues.	_____	
• The data does not exist and must be generated or created.	_____	

close—for example, if you have three factors ranked 2 and three factors ranked 6. The comments will help you decide which intensity would be the most workable in your organization.

When determining the level of intensity of your evaluation strategy, you should consider what level of effort is acceptable and balance this with the desired evaluation results. Where can time and effort for results be sacrificed, and where can the detail and quality of the results be minimized to save time, effort, and cost? It is important to understand that a low-level intensity evaluation may provide high-quality results, but with a lot less detail and information than a high-intensity evaluation. The low-intensity evaluation may thus meet the need.

Aligning the Measures With the Strategy or Intervention Objectives

In chapter 1 you identified and defined strategy objectives. Most certainly an intervention also has defined objectives. The objectives are used to validate the measurement approach and measures that have been determined at this point. This stage is a checkpoint to ensure that when the data is gathered for the measure, it will provide the necessary information regarding the results of the objective. Worksheet 2.5 illustrates how to use this information as a checkpoint with one example. If the measures do not match the measurement approach or the approach does not support the objectives, your measurement approach is not aligned, and the data you gather will not enable you to make good decisions.

In case example 2, AOK's strategy objective was to be able to evaluate instructors' performance to determine who to continue to contract with externally and to provide meaningful performance feedback to the instructor. The evaluation measurement approach included developing best practice standards from outside sources, peer assessment by instructors who taught the same material, a SME evaluation or review, and a more intensive participant feedback process. The measure was percentage of accurate technical knowledge conveyed to participants in an understandable way. The

---

Worksheet 2.5: Measure, Approach, and Objective Alignment

Strategy or Intervention Objective	Measurement Approach	Measure	Are They Aligned?
Overall strategy is to increase market position by increasing employees' product knowledge and ability to present product features and benefits and close new product sales.	Level 2: Testing for product and customer knowledge Level 3: Application of product, customer, and sales knowledge in the field Level 4: Increase sales, new product sales, cross sales Alternative method: Identification of best practices or sales training and incentive packages	Quota increase (% and $) New product sales increase (no. and $) Market share (%)	Yes
The objective is to ensure that call center employees can assist customers in troubleshooting product problems and decrease escalation to engineers	Level 2: Testing for product knowledge* Level 3: observation and telephone monitoring, call time and problem reports	Product knowledge increase* Call time decrease Customer satisfaction increase**	No

* Decrease in problem escalation is missing from measurement approach and measures.

** No approach has been identified to gather this information.

---

objective, approach, and measure are in alignment, and the results from this approach should provide meaningful information for decision making, planning, and resource development.

If you determine that the measures, strategy objectives, and approach are in alignment, then you are ready to define the parameters of the strategy and to begin to communicate your approach to gaining commitment. After reviewing the measures, objectives, and approach, if you find that something is not in alignment, then you need more research. Review the business driver and performance need to begin the continued research.

Evaluation and Measurement Review

Through the actions you took in steps 1 and 2, you defined the evaluation strategy and its corresponding measures. A final checklist (worksheet 2.6) is provided for you as a final critique of the strategy, measurement approach, and measures you have selected. In thinking about what you have developed and documented thus far, review each of the questions listed in column 1 and record in column 2 if you are satisfied with what has been done so far. If you answer "no" in column 2, document in column 3 what follow-up needs to be done so you can move forward with the strategy. This tool helps you assess whether you are ready to move to the next step: the communication and commitment

process for the evaluation strategy and measurement approach, to be discussed in chapter 3.

One Last Word

One last word on measures: It is feasible to have three to five measures and corresponding approaches for the evaluation strategy and then different approaches for specific interventions. As you consider specific intervention evaluation approaches, a key discussion point should be to determine how the specific intervention approach rolls into the evaluation strategy measures.

For example, Friendly Service Company's evaluation strategy is to use a standard reaction sheet regardless of intervention content, delivery method, or customer base. However, when a new EPSS was launched under WLP's products, the client requested that a special reaction sheet be developed to track specific functions for future development information. The EPSS evaluation sheet still used the standard questions, but questions were added and the specific information was reported under delivery method.

The specific data for the intervention should fit under the evaluation strategy umbrella. If an intervention has a completely different parameter that does not fit, it is important to ask why and to determine if the evaluation strategy may be missing an important factor or if something has changed in the environment and strategy maintenance is called for. The latter will be addressed in chapter 13.

Worksheet 2.6: Evaluation and Measurement Review Checklist

Evaluation Checklist	Are You Ready to Move to the Next Step? (Yes or No)	Necessary Follow-Up
Are the measures, measurement approach, and components of the strategy compatible?		
Are all customers defined, and have their viewpoints on evaluation been considered?		
Has a sense of balance been built into the strategy and measures from • an organizational viewpoint? • a workplace learning and performance viewpoint? • a learner viewpoint?		
Is the business linkage to the evaluation clear, and have business drivers and individual, business, and finance indicators been considered?		
Are the required resources practical for the environment?		
Is the evaluation strategy able to leverage from integration with other processes, and is that integration clear?		
Is the measurement approach able to leverage from integration with other processes, and is that integration clear?		
Can the measurement data be supported in the report process outlined by the strategy?		
Have the measurement approaches been defined and agreed to?		
Have tactics to manage measurement risk and concerns been identified and documented?		
Is the intensity of the measurement approach compatible with the evaluation strategy outcomes?		
Has the alignment of the measurement approach, evaluation strategy objectives, and measures been validated?		
Do you see any outstanding issues that need to be dealt with before communicating and gaining commitment to the strategy?		

—————————— *Chapter Summary* ——————————

This chapter addressed how to establish measures to use in evaluating a WLP strategy or intervention. It described how to validate business drivers and performance needs and identify measures from those needs. Also addressed was how to determine a measurement approach and identify issues and concerns regarding measurement. Of particular importance in this chapter was the discussion of how to determine the intensity of the measures used in an evaluation approach. Finally, how to align measures with the objectives of an evaluation strategy or an intervention was addressed.

Discussion Questions

The following questions are provided to help you apply what you learned in this chapter:

- What is a business driver, and why are business drivers important in evaluation?

  _____

  _____

- How are business drivers used in identifying measures?

  _____

  _____

- What are the three categories of measures identified in this chapter?

  _____

  _____

- What is one example of a measurement approach?

  _____

  _____

- How is Bloom's taxonomy used to identify a measurement approach?

  _____

  _____

- What are some of the issues and concerns associated with measurement, and how do they relate to your organization?

  _____

  _____

- What are the levels of measurement intensity, and why are they important?

  _____

  _____

- Why is it important for the intervention's objectives, the measurement approach, and measures to be in alignment?

  _____

  _____

References

Barksdale, Susan B., and Lund, Teri B. *How to Develop a Training Strategy—Training and Performance Sourcebook.* Edited by Mel Silberman. New York: McGraw-Hill, 1998.

Bloom, B.S. *Taxonomy of Educational Objectives: Handbook I. Cognitive Domain.* New York: David McKay, 1956.

Kirkpatrick, Donald L. *Evaluating Training Programs.* San Francisco: Berrett-Koehler Publishers, 1994.

Communicating and Gaining Commitment to the Strategy

*E*valuation strategies often fail because they are not communicated properly or commitment to the strategy is not gained up front. Being a strong communicator and having the ability to influence others are two of the key skills of an evaluator.

In our world of competing priorities, fast-paced decision making, and Internet speed, the term *strategic planning* often translates to acquiring more information than needed to create plans that sit on a shelf (not to mention that *evaluation* often means spending needless time proving there was a reason for one's existence). Instead, it needs to be demonstrated that strategic planning for evaluation means identifying actions that will allocate resources toward gathering meaningful data so that decisions can be made quickly and accountability for products and services taken.

This chapter describes

- case examples illustrating how to communicate and gain commitment to evaluation strategies
- communicating and gaining commitment to the strategy and the results that will be realized on implementation
- building champions for implementing the strategy by using political savvy and influence
- meeting the ongoing need for communication and influence.

Case Examples

Case Example 1

Apex Manufacturing Company created an expansive yet precise evaluation strategy. When the WLP leadership identified the people who would need only to understand the contents versus those who would need to commit to the goals and authorize the implementation, they ended up with lists that were quite different. Consequently, they identified two very different communication needs—a political mine field.

Aware that it was important that those who needed only to know what was happening also felt included in the decision-making process, WLP management identified milestones in the evaluation strategy development where feedback would be meaningful. They created an interactive Website dedicated to the strategy's development, enabling them to communicate with more than 1,000 managers at the same time. The WLP leadership then used the feedback solicited via the Website to strengthen the overall plan. This communication cycle did not lengthen the time to develop the plan because of the mechanism used to communicate. The capability was already there (a Website was available), and Website review was a commonly used method in the organization.

When the plan was completed, WLP management met with those who would authorize the strategy. The senior managers were well informed in part because their managers had communicated how positive the process was and were champions for the overall strategy.

Case Example 2

Computer Software Solutions delivers training to its customer base globally. Because its customers perceived its WLP products and services as separate, paid-for services, management was concerned that if the services provided did not meet customers' expectations, it would influence their future buying decisions. Consequently, it asked WLP to monitor, evaluate, and be accountable for the quality of its products and services.

Early on it was clear there were four primary stakeholders in the evaluation strategy and implementation:

1. the senior manager of marketing
2. the senior manager of sales
3. the senior manager of product development
4. the senior manager of customer relations.

Because time (as always) was of the essence, the strategy was communicated with the four senior managers and their commitment gained at key intervals so that when the final strategy was delivered, it took minimal time to gain commitments.

Communicating and Gaining Commitment

The two case examples demonstrate how radically different business cultures can be and how the resultant evaluation strategy communication and commitment buy-in differ. It is important to assess what the communication need is and how to gain commitment very early in the development of the strategy so that time isn't wasted on re-work for the strategy or in "selling" the strategy to those who misunderstand its purpose or goals.

Gaining commitment relies on being prepared to discuss the strategy, the outcomes of the strategy, the resources for implementation, and what to expect. Consequently, you should spend some time on creating a communication plan during the process of creating the evaluation strategy. Worksheet 3.1 can help you formulate a thorough communication plan for your or your customer's organization.

Four key actions are involved in communicating an evaluation strategy and gaining commitment to it: 1) identifying sponsors, 2) identifying constraints, 3) stating the benefits, and 4) articulating the negative consequences of nonaction.

Identifying Sponsors

The first step is to identify the sponsors, stakeholders, and users of the information the strategy will generate. Some questions to consider as you begin to gain commitment for the evaluation strategy include the following:

- Who has the most to gain or lose from implementing the evaluation strategy?
- How will the results be used, and who will benefit (and how) from the information from the evaluation strategy deliverables?
- Who wants the evaluation to be used, and why?
- Who does not want the evaluation used, and why?
- Who or what will be the sources of information for the evaluation data, and will they be accessible?
- What records or other information might prove useful?
- How much organizational support do evaluation principles have overall?
- What levels within the organization support implementing an evaluation strategy?
- Who needs to know about the evaluation findings, and why?

Identifying Constraints

Find out not only who does not agree with developing or implementing an evaluation strategy, but why. Become knowledgeable about resource constraints and the politics surrounding the situation. Constraints may include

- fear of evaluation results
- previous experience with a poorly executed evaluation project
- budget or other lack of resources
- lack of understanding of the benefits of evaluation.

Stating the Benefits

Articulate the need for the evaluation strategy in business terms and state the benefits of the strategy as related to business results. "Selling" the need for the strategy with benefits is particularly effective if done from the customers' perspective—what's in it for them to have the evaluation strategy implemented. Benefits may include

- better information for decision making
- clearer understanding of what to improve and how
- performance information
- customers feeling valued because you "care" what they think
- earlier identification of problems.

Articulating the Negative Consequences of Nonaction

Being clear about the consequences of not implementing an evaluation strategy will help you gain commitment to it. Such consequences may include money spent on the wrong interventions; interventions that don't solve performance problems; customer apathy or dissatisfaction; loss of competitive advantage; incorrect allocation of resources; and inability to spot trends and issues before they become critical.

Building Champions for the Strategy

John F. Kennedy once said, "Mothers may still want their favorite sons to grow up to be President, but they do not want them to become politicians in the process" (*American Heritage Dictionary*, 1978, p. 1015). The word *politics* is often considered a negative term, yet

Worksheet 3.1: Communication Plan Worksheet

Content Considerations	Notes Specific to Organization
Mission and Purpose • What is the purpose of the evaluation strategy? • What is important to the organization about the evaluation strategy? • What is important to WLP about implementing the evaluation strategy? • What is the focus of the evaluation strategy? • What is the business linkage of the evaluation strategy? • What are the results or outcomes of the evaluation strategy?	
Measures • What will the measurement approach be? • How will the measurement approach be balanced? • What is important about the approach in terms of individual, business, and financial considerations? • How will the data from the measures assist in improving WLP products and services?	
Evaluation Structure and Scope Definition • What will be considered part of the evaluation strategy products, processes, and services? • What will be considered *not* part of the evaluation strategy products, processes, or services?	
Integration with Other Processes • What processes will the evaluation strategy integrate with, and how will the strategy complement the other processes?	
Roles and Accountabilities • Who is the owner of the evaluation strategy? • What do those being communicated with expect regarding the evaluation strategy?	
Resource Requirements • What are the resource requirements for the evaluation strategy? • How will these resources be approved? Is approval needed for the resource requirements? What is the approval process?	
Next Steps • Who needs to take action? • What actions need to be taken? • What is the time frame? • When can results be expected?	

gaining commitment to plans, projects, and products usually involves politics. *Being political* should instead be equated with getting things done. And to get things done, you must be influential.

Influence is crucial in gaining commitment to an evaluation strategy. Frequently there are many stakeholders in an evaluation strategy—the data owner, the customer, the WLP professionals, and others. Most often, to gain access to the necessary information for evaluation, you must rely on others who control either the data or the resources controlling the data. This fact, in dynamic competitive environments, means that there is protection around data and knowledge that can make commitment to and implementation of an evaluation strategy much more complicated.

Understanding the basic principles of influence is important and using those principles to influence the commitment to an evaluation strategy is essential. The following steps can help you build your influence with key players:

1. Identify the main benefits of the evaluation strategy in furthering competitive advantage from the perspectives of the individual, the customer, the business, and the learning environment.

2. Define the need for an evaluation strategy and demonstrate how it can be done efficiently and effectively using as few resources as possible for the greatest results.

3. Create concise statements about the evaluation strategy (evaluation key messages) that take into consideration the stakeholders' and sponsors' concerns and goals.

4. Lay a solid foundation of what the results from the evaluation strategy will provide the organization (and the stakeholders and sponsors) by articulating clearly and specifically its purpose and objectives.

5. Recognize those who control the necessary resources and demonstrate respect for their control.

Finally, to gain influence, you must be an authority. Learn as much about how the evaluation strategy results can be used, how the strategy will promote strong business practices, and the benefits of evaluation so you come across as an expert.

Ongoing Need for Communication and Influence

The need for communication and influence does not stop at gaining commitment for the evaluation strategy but continues throughout the evaluation process. In many situations, communication and influence are critical skills in gaining or maintaining commitment to an evaluation strategy. The following are specific examples:

- You are trying to demonstrate an ROI for the intervention and need the previous costs to identify the benefit the intervention provided. The finance group knows the costs for the process that was in place prior to a WLP intervention but is reluctant to release this information because of concerns about how it will be used.

- A group of 20 individuals agreed to provide transfer-to-the-job information but now are too busy to attend a focus group. They all say they are using the knowledge and that the intervention was very valuable, but they just don't have an hour to give to you to quantify the gains.

- A best practices company is concerned that you will not handle its data in a confidential manner and is not willing to give you the information you need for a comparison study.

Before asking for information or resources, you should think about what specifically you are asking for. Sometimes a little preparation and communication can go a long way in getting what you need to make the evaluation a success. The evaluation sales process in worksheet 3.2 may help you wield influence in carrying out the evaluation strategy.

Worksheet 3.2: Evaluation Sales Process

Preparing to Influence	Your Notes
What is the request? Be as concise as possible and describe exactly what you need from the other person.	
What are the benefits to the people involved? Will they get information that is usable to them? Will they demonstrate their ability to be team players? Will they provide the organization an invaluable service?	
What is the likely resistance to the request? (Examples are, "Not enough time." "Don't have the requested information." "Aren't sure why *you* need this information.")	
How can you overcome the resistance? Volunteer to look through the files yourself. Share the report with the data provider. Provide the data provider with a resource (administrative or other) to assist with other work while he or she helps you. Invite the data provider to lunch.	
What follow-up or closure do you need to ensure that you get what you need after agreement to provide you with the necessary support? A meeting, a phone call, or picking up the information yourself may be necessary.	

Chapter Summary

The focus of this chapter was on how to communicate the need for an evaluation strategy and how to influence others so that you gain commitment to developing and implementing the strategy. A communication process and plan were presented and the basic principles for influencing a commitment outlined. Finally, an evaluation sales process was outlined for preparing a case for an evaluation strategy.

Discussion Questions

The following discussion questions are provided to help you apply what you learned in this chapter:

- What are the key actions involved in communicating the need for an evaluation strategy?

  _____

  _____

- How would you use the communication plan worksheet (worksheet 3.1) to prepare for communicating the need for an evaluation strategy?

  _____

  _____

- Why is the ability to influence so critical to gaining commitment to an evaluation strategy?

  _____

  _____

- Why does the need for communicating and influencing continue after you gain commitment to the strategy?

  _____

  _____

- What are the steps in the evaluation sales process, and how would you use the process in your organization?

  _____

  _____

Reference

American Heritage Dictionary. Boston: Houghton-Mifflin, 1978.

Developing Level 1 (Reaction) Tools

Level 1 (Reaction) is the most misunderstood and underused evaluation level. It is often referred to as a "smile sheet," because often Level 1 evaluation entails only a survey completed immediately after the training that yields positive, rather than constructive, feedback. In some companies it is the only evaluation level implemented, and the tools used for the approach are meaningless. The data is taken, filed away, and never reviewed or used again. It also wastes time, especially that of your customer or the participant or user who takes the time to complete it. All of this gives evaluation a bad name.

Fortunately, some companies have taken the time to ask:

1. Is Level 1 evaluation worthwhile for us?

2. Will we use this type of data?

3. If we don't want evaluation at this level, can we implement a Level 3 (Transfer) evaluation?

4. If we do want evaluation at this level, what data would be of most value, and when?

5. What items should be on the "reaction sheet"?

6. Are there other ways to gather this type of data?

7. Would those methods be a better fit in our organization?

This chapter provides a process for you to determine what (if any) Level 1 information should be collected in your or your customer's organization and, if so, how. The following information regarding Level 1 evaluation is presented:

- defining Level 1 evaluation
- case examples illustrating the use of Level 1 evaluation
- determining if Level 1 evaluation is needed
- selecting measurement intensity
- building a Level 1 low-intensity tool

- building a Level 1 moderate-intensity tool
- building a Level 1 high-intensity tool.

Defining Level 1 Evaluation

Donald Kirkpatrick (1994) developed a model for evaluation in the late 1950s that has been used continually since then (with adaptations and modifications). This model provides a framework for evaluating programs and services aimed at improving workplace learning and performance. The model comprises four levels:

- Level 1—Reaction, which will be defined and discussed in this chapter
- Level 2—Learning (chapter 5)
- Level 3—Behavior/Transfer (chapter 6)
- Level 4—Results (chapter 7).

The purpose of the first level is to provide information on participant or user satisfaction with the intervention. Level 1 evaluation seeks answers to the question, Was this experience satisfactory, and did it meet your needs? Not only WLP professionals use this type of information. The same evaluation level is used by restaurants, hotels, banks, stores, and other businesses that decide that this type of information would be helpful in improving products and services through a systematic approach that can be documented and measured.

All four levels are important to WLP and should be considered as mechanisms to gain critical information to manage programs, products, and services. Realistically, however, not all four levels need to be implemented for each and every program, product, or service. It is important for you to understand what each level will yield so your or your customer's organization implements the tools that will provide the best information for its evaluation needs.

Case Examples

Case Example 1

RLB Corporate University had a reaction sheet in place, but many of the participants in its courses complained that the reaction sheet took too much time at the end of an event to complete. Statistically, the data was called into question because many of those who completed the sheet marked all items with the same answer (e.g., all 3s on a scale of 5 to 1). Finally, a review of the use of the reports generated from the data revealed that few of those on the distribution list looked at the information.

In response to these complaints, the university's evaluation team determined that two reaction sheets would be developed. The first would consist of eight questions and would allow for comments. It would be used for 95 percent of the programs or events.

The second reaction sheet would consist of 20 questions. It would be used on a random basis to assess each program at least once a year and each instructor at least once a quarter. It would also be used if an exception to the trends for a course occurred. The longer questionnaire included the eight questions from the short questionnaire and 12 others that asked for more information on the content, the instructor, the facilities and logistics, and registration.

After using both questionnaires for a year, the evaluation team noticed that a contract instructor who had worked for the university for over five years with great success was suddenly getting lower ratings and a few remarks about inappropriate behavior. Their review of the lengthy questionnaire responses revealed that, as he always had, he had told controversial stories in class; however, as the mix of students grew, the stories became less acceptable. The manager of the university spoke with the instructor, who had not realized that his stories offended some of the students, and the behavior stopped. This approach provided the university with the information needed to improve quality, and it also provided participants with a voice in managing the quality.

Case Example 2

The WLP group in Business Professionals Association had used a standard reaction sheet for a long time. The products and services they supported and offered, however, had changed over the years. Whereas previously they offered mostly training courses and instructor-led interventions, now they provided electronic performance support systems (EPSSs), a variety of on-the-job training products, Web-facilitated training, and consulting on projects for competency design or team building. Did they really need a reaction sheet? Was it appropriate?

After a lengthy discussion, the WLP department decided that there was a great deal of value in knowing if their services and products had met expectations. Sending a short questionnaire or providing one online as part of "the package" sent a message to customers that their feedback was valued, especially on future needs, and that they wanted the customers to return. The WLP group created a new reaction sheet with five questions (including, Would you use our services or products again?) that was standardized for all services and products.

Case Example 3

Tech ONE, which provides performance and learning products to customers outside of the organization, used a reaction sheet. The company was a global institution with numerous sites in Canada and the United States, Malaysia, Australia, England, France, Germany, Mexico, Brazil, and Argentina. When developing an evaluation strategy, management discovered that not only was the reaction sheet outdated (e.g., it did not apply to alternate delivery methods that did not use an instructor), it missed needed data and was not adaptable. Occasionally one of the foreign offices or product groups wanted additional information from the reaction sheet, but there was no way to use this vehicle for anything but its traditional 10 questions.

The organization revised its reaction sheet and developed an online version that was emailed to its customers. Each group manager had the ability to modify it and ask three different questions, the responses to which could be collated and reported through the system. In addition, it was possible to generate specific ad hoc reports and compare information not routinely compared in the commonly distributed reports. The system is popular with the company's managers, but customer management likes it too because they can obtain information that helps them make future training decisions.

Is Level 1 Evaluation Needed?

When considering Level 1 evaluation, the first question you should ask is, Will we use data from a Level 1 reaction sheet? Worksheet 4.1 provides a set of criteria to use in thinking through whether Level 1 data is the best for your or your customer's organization. In reviewing the responses to worksheet 4.1, ask yourself, How do my responses reflect the organization's business goals and values? Would a Level 1 reaction sheet contribute to how the company presents itself? For example, if the organization is extremely customer oriented and "walks the talk," you should have more yes than no responses.

So when do you *not* use a Level 1 evaluation? The answer: When you are not going to use the data. Other methods may be needed to provide the most valuable data for the organization. Deploying a reaction sheet

---

Worksheet 4.1: Is a Level 1 Reaction Sheet the Best Tool?

Yes	No	Level 1 Criterion Question
☐	☐	Is it important for you to know if you have met your customers' expectations?
☐	☐	Do you need to know how customers perceived the product, service, event, or program?
☐	☐	Do you want to track trends and changes by program, product, or service?
☐	☐	Do you want to identify improvement opportunities for your program, product, or service?
☐	☐	Do you want problems to surface quickly and to be able to react to them before they become a delivery problem?
☐	☐	Are you moving to new technology, new services, or new techniques and want to know which are better accepted by your customers and why?
☐	☐	Do you need consistent data across geographic lines for programs, services, and product offerings?
☐	☐	Will you take appropriate action if an issue surfaces?
☐	☐	Will you be able to provide timely access to the data so that it is meaningful and can be used?
☐	☐	Will you be able to interpret and summarize the comments and suggestions so they can be used in dentifying trends, future needs, issues, and concerns?

---

because it looks like you care about what the customer thinks is not good business. If you follow that tactic, it won't be long before someone writes a comment that is not responded to, and the word will be out: The reaction sheet is just a smile sheet, and no one cares what is said.

The most important question to ask when designing a reaction sheet is, What do you want to find out? Collecting what will not be used is wasteful and time-consuming. So of all the things that can be captured as part of a Level 1 tool, which will meet the business needs defined in the evaluation strategy? Table 4.1 can help you determine what types of data should be gathered from a Level 1 evaluation.

Selecting Measurement Intensity

The concept of measurement intensity was presented in chapter 2, where it was defined as the extent of effort or the amount of information needed. The three levels of intensity were identified as low, moderate, and high. Examples of Level 1 tools and types of data are compared at the different intensities in table 4.2.

To identify which Level 1 measurement intensity is best for you or your customer's needs, compare those needs to the statements in table 4.3.

Building a Low-Intensity Tool

The most difficult part of developing a Level 1 low-intensity tool is coming to an agreement on what it will and will not include. Table 4.1 showed that there are many data components that can be assessed in a low-intensity tool. Development of a low-intensity tool consists of a series of general steps:

1. Determine the purposes the tool will serve. Will it be used only for stand-up instruction? Will it be online only? Will it be used for WLP products and services both?

2. Determine the format or media that will be used to present and track the results. Will it be paper only or online, or both?

3. Select the items that are important to the business to track and that will help maintain the quality of WLP products and services (review your responses in worksheet 4.1).

4. Determine what ranking or rating scale will be used. The most common is a five-point scale where 5 is "excellent," "high," or "strongly agree" and 1 is "poor," "low," or "strongly disagree."

Table 4.1: Level 1 Data Components

Type of Data	Reason for Gathering	Data Components
Logistics	Facility change Facility complaint Customer satisfaction Critical to solution effectiveness	Room Location Comfort (e.g., chairs, setup, heat) Access to telephones, PCs, and other equipment
Instructor	Performance data Complaints Contractors New instructor New material	Instructor ability Content knowledge and expertise Speaker or presenter ability Relationship to participants
Participant demographics	Class or position match Type of background vs. needs assessment Trends in attendance Future planning	Position Education background Experience background Time on job Length of company experience Reason for attendance
Value of learning solution	Alignment with business Future planning Marketing Pricing	Alignment with business application Why learning solution was selected Effectiveness of solution Repeat business Differentiation from competition Input into business strategies Customer satisfaction Cost and value information
Media	New media Comparison of types of media (classroom vs. Web) Effectiveness	Media effectiveness Timeliness Applicability to content
Practice and labs	Effectiveness Transferability to job Level 2 evaluation component	Applicability to content Similarity to job Effectiveness
Future needs	Planning	Effectiveness Alignment with present need Future need
Marketing and registration	Source of enrollment Decision-making process Pricing Ease of registration	Source of enrollment Decision-making process Pricing Registration process
Open comments	Other data Opportunity to identify unknown evaluation needs	Other comments

Table 4.2: Comparison of Level 1 Measurement Intensities

Characteristic	Low Intensity	Moderate Intensity	High Intensity
Tool examples	Undefined Likert Scale (allows for interpretation) Open-ended questions in a survey	Anchored survey statements that leave little to no room for interpretation Specific questions tied to content, delivery, or value	Interviews or focus groups with participants or managers postcourse Specific interview questioning script
Type of data gathered	Broad data not tied to specific planning, quality, or customer satisfaction objectives. For example, "Did this course meet your expectation?" (yes or no)	Data tied to specific planning, quality, and customer satisfaction objectives. For example, "You attended this course with the objective of learning to develop behavioral interviewing questions. Did the course assist you in meeting this objective?" (yes or no)	Data tied to specific planning, quality, and customer satisfaction objectives. For example, "You attended this course with the objective of learning to develop behavioral interviewing questions. Explain how the course did or did not meet this objective."

Table 4.3: Determining the Intensity of Your Level 1 Evaluation Needs

Intensity Level	Which set of characteristics will most closely meet your needs?
Low intensity	We need to identify trends. The tool needs to be easy to administer across groups and countries. The tool needs to be easy to create. Data needs to be collected using a simple system (e.g., Excel or Access). Resources are limited. Participants' time is limited. Information will be used over a period of time.
Moderate intensity	We need the data to leave little to no room for interpretation. The tool needs to be easy to administer across groups and countries. We can tolerate more difficulty in creating the tool. We are able to analyze more complex data. Evaluation and analysis resources are available, as is appropriate training. Participants' time is limited. Information needs to be specific and targeted (e.g., anchored rating scale or specific focus group information).
High intensity	We need to focus on a short-term need for detailed information (e.g., we have a product concern or are piloting an intervention). The tool must be easily adapted or probed for more information as needed. We can tolerate more complexity in creating the tool. We are able to analyze more complex data. Evaluation and analysis resources are available, as is appropriate training. Participants' time is available as needed. We need information that is specific to time period and situation.

5. Identify what, if any, demographics are needed (e.g., length of time with company, position, department), but keep an eye on confidentiality. If you ask for the position and only two people are in that position, then confidentiality will be compromised.

6. Determine how you want open comments and suggestions to be captured (e.g., as part of each question or at the bottom of the survey).

7. Identify the degree of flexibility the tool needs. Will it need to be automated for use with Web programs or computer-based training? Will it need to be adapted to other countries or languages?

8. Determine how the tool will be distributed (email, online, in person at the end of a program, in a postproject conference).

9. Determine how the results will be tracked, monitored, and reported.

10. Determine how the results will be communicated to the participants, users, and others.

The items you include in a low-intensity Level 1 tool should meet certain standard criteria for ease of use and analysis; worksheet 4.2 lists those criteria. Tool 4.1 provides an example of a low-intensity Level 1 tool.

Building a Moderate-Intensity Tool

You can use the process for developing a low-intensity tool to develop a moderate-intensity tool, with the following modifications:

- The items and the responses need to be quantitative and should provide little to no room for interpretation.

- The analysis of the items becomes more important because the instruments are less open to interpretation. Data discrepancies need to be identified and possibly researched. The analysis is more quantitative in nature and requires validation.

- Open-ended comment sections need to be validated with the anchor to ensure consistency and identify potential data discrepancies. In moderate-intensity Level 1 evaluation, items should not be left open to interpretation. So, for example, in evaluating the content of courseware, you might ask, How can the content be improved (more technical information, additional exercises)? In this way you "anchor" the response.

The intensity of the instrument is in the item design and ranking, as well as the analysis and interpretation. Tool 4.2 is an example of a moderate-inten-

---

Worksheet 4.2: Standard Criteria for Low-Intensity Level 1 Items

Criterion for Level 1 Items	Example	Yes	No
The item is concise and has fewer than 10 words.	The handouts will be helpful to me.		
Each item has only one topic for evaluation.	The content was useful (*not* The content was useful and the instructor technically competent).		
The wording was chosen with care. If the tool is to be used in other countries, the items mean the same when translated to that culture.	The logistics did not detract from learning (*not* The logistics were good).		
The rating matches the item.	Rank the item 5 = strongly agree to 1 = strongly disagree (*not* Answer yes or no).		
Items were designed to quantify reactions.	The instructor provides the appropriate level of technical information (*not* The instructor met my needs).		

Tool 4.1: Sample Level 1 Low-Intensity Reaction Sheet

Instructions: Circle the appropriate response to each statement and add any comments you have about the training below.

	Strongly Agree		Agree		Strongly Disagree
The content will be useful in my job.	5	4	3	2	1
The instructor was an effective communicator.	5	4	3	2	1
The audiovisual aids were effective.	5	4	3	2	1
The registration process was easy.	5	4	3	2	1
I would recommend this course to others.	5	4	3	2	1

Comments:

_____

_____

_____

sity tool that uses anchors to rate the responses and solicits comments in response to each question.

Building a High-Intensity Tool

High-intensity Level 1 tools typically are used when a concern, new need, or change arises or when an intervention is piloted and more information is needed about its quality, delivery method, service, and product. High-intensity Level 1 tools include very specific items; they are not as general or broad as low- and moderate-intensity items. A high-intensity Level 1 evaluation for a pilot training would most likely focus on the content, structure, exercises, and activities and probably not on the instructor (a low-intensity evaluation could be paired with the high-intensity tool to get instructor information).

High-intensity tools are also used in facilitated interviews or focus groups. They are most commonly guided scripts to gain specific evaluation information that is needed for a point in time. If a problem arises with an instructor, or navigation in a course seems to be confusing, then a short focus group may save a

great deal of time in discovering the problem and getting to the solution that will improve the intervention. Tool 4.3 provides an example of a high-intensity tool comprising questions for use with interviews of focus groups in evaluating a pilot course.

An effective high-intensity Level 1 tool must have the following characteristics:

- Both complimentary and contrary follow-up cues must be written so the evaluation yields both favorable and negative feedback. If contrary cues are not identified, you may end up with one-sided feedback and audience bias and confusion. If complimentary cues are not used, you may give the impression that the contrary feedback is what you are seeking and inadvertently lead the audience.

- Questions may need to be designed that validate or counter the data previously collected in another type of Level 1 tool (such as a low-intensity reaction sheet).

- The focus group or interview questions should meet standard evaluation criteria, outlined in worksheet 4.3.

Tool 4.2: Sample Level 1 Moderate-Intensity Reaction Sheet

Instructions: Check only one possible response for each multiple choice question (1-4) and explain why you chose that response. Please provide comments for questions 5-7.

1. What was the value of the case studies?
   - ❏ The case studies simulated real work world.
   - ❏ The case studies paralleled my job.
   - ❏ I may use concepts back on the job.
   - ❏ The case studies did not reinforce content.

   Why? _____

2. What was the value of the seminar to your time?
   - ❏ Value exceeded time
   - ❏ Value was equal to time
   - ❏ Value was less than time

   Why? _____

3. Do you perceive that one of the following barriers to applying what you learned in this seminar will be present once you get back to the job?
   - ❏ No time
   - ❏ Lack of adequate resources
   - ❏ No support group
   - ❏ Lack of management support
   - ❏ Other: _____

   Why? _____

4. What will you do when you return to the job to ensure that you apply what you have learned? (Please check all that apply.)
   - ❏ Meet with my manager
   - ❏ Set goals for myself
   - ❏ Talk with others who took the class
   - ❏ Review the key concepts
   - ❏ Other: _____

   Why? _____

5. Seminar strengths: What was most valuable to you?

   _____

   _____

6. Seminar weaknesses: What would you recommend to improve the seminar?

   _____

   _____

7. Other comments:

   _____

   _____

Tool 4.3: Sample High-Intensity Evaluation Questions for Interviews and Focus Groups for a Pilot Course for Supervisory Orientation

Element of Course	Question	Complimentary Feedback	Contrary Feedback
Content	How did the content compare to your expectations of the course?	What role did you play in the group and in the disagreement resolution?	Did you take responsibility for arbitrating disagreements?
		Was there resolution for the group? Did the group reach a decision or outcome?	Did you focus a group on business objectives and coming to a consensus for the "bigger picture"?
		What process did you follow or actions did you take in identifying or resolving issues for the group? How did you do this? Be specific.	Did you identify and proactively resolve issues?
Structure	How did the structure and sequencing of the content contribute to or detract from your learning experience?	What parts of the course content seemed to transition especially well? Why?	What parts of the course content seemed disjointed and confusing?
		Was there any part of the course that you felt was particularly well structured? Why?	Did any part of the course seem to fall apart? Why did you feel that it did?
		Are there any parts of the course you feel should definitely stay in the same order as they were presented?	Are there any parts of the course that you felt were out of order and should be changed? What order would you recommend?
Exercises and activities	How did the exercises and activities compare to the types of situations you run into in your job day to day?	Was there an exercise or activity that you felt was particularly meaningful or job related? Why or how?	Were some of the exercises or activities confusing or unrelated to what you do day to day?
		Which exercise or activity provided the most meaningful scenario? How? Why did you think this?	How could the exercises and activities be improved and provide more realistic scenarios?
		What exercises or activities would you recommend absolutely be kept in the course, and why?	Did any of the exercises or activities seem wasteful or unnecessary?
		What debrief was the most meaningful, and why?	How could the debriefs of exercises be improved on?

Worksheet 4.3: Standard Criteria for High-Intensity Level 1 Items

Check If the Evaluation Questions Meet the Criterion	Criterion
☐	The question is brief and clear.
☐	The question requires the respondent to reflect on specifics from a WLP product or service that is being evaluated and not "in general."
☐	The question is appropriate to the audience.
☐	The question is open ended.
☐	The question links to the complimentary and contrary cues in an obvious way.
☐	The question does not lead the respondents.
☐	The question does not contain vocabulary that is unrelated or appears to be WLP jargon to the respondent.
☐	Technical terminology used relates specifically to the product or service being evaluated.
☐	Auxiliary verbs such as *could, might, will,* and *would* are not used (these words are conditional and open to interpretation).

Chapter Summary

This chapter has demonstrated that Level 1 tools take different forms and vary according to business need. The key to making reaction more meaningful than a smile sheet is to determine what you really want to find out about your customer's perception of the WLP products, services, and programs you offer.

In this chapter, Level 1 (Reaction) was defined and criteria for when to use it presented. The data components for Level 1 were identified, along with a process for developing tools to evaluate at this level. The characteristics of low-, moderate-, and high-intensity measurements for Level 1 were listed and examples of tools for each level of intensity provided.

Discussion Questions

The following questions are provided to help you apply what you learned in this chapter:

- What is Level 1 evaluation?

_____

_____

- When is a Level 1 evaluation needed?

_____

_____

- What type of reaction information is needed in your or your customer's organization?

  _____

  _____

- When would you use a low-intensity Level 1 tool?

  _____

  _____

- When would you use a moderate-intensity Level 1 tool?

  _____

  _____

- When would you use a high-intensity Level 1 tool?

  _____

  _____

  _____

Reference

Kirkpatrick, Donald. *Evaluating Training Programs.* San Francisco: Berrett-Koehler Publishers, 1994.

Developing Level 2 (Learning) Tools

evel 2 (Learning) is usually equated with testing, but in actuality there are numerous ways besides testing to determine if an employee has actually learned something new. The purpose of Level 2 is really to determine if

- the participant acquired knowledge, or now knows something he or she did not before the intervention
- the participant developed or enhanced skills, or can do something he or she could not before the intervention
- the participant's thought process has changed, or he or she believes something different following the intervention.

You can evaluate "learning" in a variety of ways, and measuring learning is a time-consuming and sometimes very difficult task. It takes a great deal more specialized knowledge and expertise than it does to measure reaction. In this chapter, the following information regarding Level 2 is presented:

- defining Level 2 evaluation
- case examples illustrating how Level 2 has been used
- determining if Level 2 is needed
- describing Level 2 measurement intensity
- building a Level 2 low-intensity tool
- building a Level 2 moderate-intensity tool
- building a Level 2 high-intensity tool.

Defining Level 2 Evaluation

The intent of Level 2 is to ensure that learning has resulted from a WLP intervention. This could mean that an employee is more confident in answering customer questions regarding claims and insurance adjustments because of the electronic performance support system (EPSS), or another employee may now have a better understanding of how networks function because of a Web-based course. Level 2 does not measure what one does with the learning; only that it occurred. Table 5.1 lists three examples of interventions along with a learning objective and evaluation method for each, and the various types of Level 2 learning assessments are described in table 5.2.

To evaluate at Level 2, you will need to engage in some sort of measurement both beforehand, to establish what the employee knows or understands, and following the intervention, to show that the employee as a result understands how, and most likely is able, to perform the task. Consequently, the following must occur for measurement at Level 2:

- The learning must be tied to the objectives and content of the intervention. If there is no content related to the objectives, then one cannot validate that the learning resulted from the intervention. Likewise, the intervention must be tied to the performance gap.
- Before the intervention takes place, it is important to assess participants' performance and identify the performance gap that the intervention will resolve.
- A postintervention analysis (e.g., test, observation) should be conducted to determine if the employee now performs at the desired level in a safe environment (not necessarily back on the job) and the performance gap has been closed. It is desirable, but not required, to have the preassessment and postassessment measured with the same tool, administered once before and once after the intervention.

Table 5.3 demonstrates the various methods of assessing an employee's learning and illustrates the close relationship between Level 2 evaluation and Bloom's taxonomy. By matching the verbs listed in the first column with the learning or performance objectives of the intervention, you can see the variety of learning assessments that can complement Level 2 evaluation.

Table 5.1: How to Evaluate Learning

Learning Objective	Intervention	Evaluation
To be able to recall new product information	A marketing seminar that introduces the new products, the features and benefits, and how they compare to the competition	During a role play, the participant is asked what new products have been introduced and how they compare to the competition.
To be able to operate a line machine that creates aluminum parts for new chips	A one-on-one, on-the-job training session using the equipment	A structured observation checklist is used by the instructor to monitor the participant to ensure that the work is done correctly.
To be able to not "make assumptions" about others because of their appearance	Diversity awareness training	An individual dressed much like a homeless person wanders into the class during lunch break and asks for directions. Afterward, the instructor asks the participants who they think the individual was or what he or she really wanted.

Table 5.2: Types of Level 2 Learning Assessment Tools

Level 2 Learning Assessment Tool	Characteristic
Oral questions	Determines understanding as information is presented Is an informal method that provides immediate feedback Provides a knowledge checkpoint
Performance tests	Assesses performance against objectives Determines if an employee can perform a specific task Pinpoints specific difficulties encountered by the employee Measures ability to perform procedure or implement a process
Performance checklist	Compares performance against a set of expected standards Provides a specific list of behaviors or task processes to measure task effectiveness Provides coaching tool and immediate task feedback
Observation	Provides immediate feedback Assesses performance of a skill or task Provides measurement of practical application by the employee Indicates whether the individual has sufficient skills, knowledge, or behavior change to apply learning back on the job
Written test	Measures knowledge base or attitudinal skill Measures the employee's ability to identify a process or step through matching or ranking Measures if the employee can discriminate between two or more choices Determines generalized understanding of the material presented in the intervention
Follow-up interviews	Measures knowledge base Allows the employee to discuss application of learning back on the job Allows for follow-up questions

Table 5.3: Bloom's Taxonomy and Low-Intensity Level 2 Assessment Types

Domain	Complementary Assessment Type
Knowledge (Domain 1) Assesses the ability to recall, define, recognize, repeat, memorize, match, list, state, write, cite	Structured game exercise—an interactive set of problems, questions, or situations (done with a computer or other learners) that leads to one or a variety of content and skill demonstrations True/false test—a series of items with only two responses; this is effective only if content is naturally dichotomous and requires more thought at a higher cognitive level so that participants are not likely to guess the answer Multiple-choice test—each item provides a variety of answers from which the learner must select the correct one Matching test—two lists of items among which the learner must determine the linkages
Comprehension (Domain 2) Assesses the ability to translate, categorize, segregate, select, sort, discuss, recognize, identify, review, restate, interpret, classify, describe, distinguish, express, indicate, locate, tell, summarize	Simulations—activities (usually video or computer based) that mimic the work environment, allowing the learner to resolve problems using the knowledge and skills gained from the solution Matching test Structured game exercise Case studies—a story-like device that forces the learner to work through key and superfluous information to identify a specific outcome or needed data point Structured role play—a role play set up with specific guidelines that should result in a specific outcome or result Scenario—a description of a work-like situation that a learner must decipher to determine the necessary result or information True/false test Multiple-choice test
Application (Domain 3) Assesses the ability to apply, use, solve, demonstrate, explain, teach, illustrate, show, sketch, schedule, operate, prepare, interpret, choose, determine	Simulations Matching test Structured game exercise Case studies Structured role play Scenario True/false test Multiple-choice test
Analysis (Domain 4) Assesses the ability to analyze, differentiate, discriminate, inspect, probe, adapt, compare, diagram, test, question, experiment, examine, distinguish, perceive	Simulations Matching test Structured game exercise
Synthesis (Domain 5) Assesses the ability to arrange, organize, plan, synthesize, create, design, formulate, construct, propose, prepare, develop, improve, integrate, merge	Simulations Case studies Structured role play Scenario Structured game exercise

(continued next page)

Table 5.3: Bloom's Taxonomy and Low-Intensity Level 2 Assessment Types *(continued)*

Domain	Complementary Assessment Type
Evaluation (Domain 6) Assesses the ability to appraise, choose, select, value, predict, assess, estimate, evaluate, decide	Simulations Case studies Scenario Structured word problems—a problem is defined with possible solutions and processes; the individual must select the appropriate solution and the appropriate process to reach that solution Structured game exercise

Bloom, B.S. *Taxonomy of Educational Objectives: Handbook I. Cognitive Domain.* New York: David McKay, 1956.

Although evaluation at Level 2 provides no indication whether the employee will use the information on the job, evaluating at Level 2 is satisfactory for some purposes. It is used in certification programs, where the goal is to ensure that learning did take place, and it is often required in licensing and regulatory situations.

Case Examples

Case Example 1

Software Etc. had developed short written tests for each of its International Standards Organization (ISO) certification courses. However, because curriculum offerings had increased, the company was finding that maintaining the tests and ensuring that each was legally defensible and usable had become a burden. In reviewing their Level 2 evaluation needs, they decided to identify other ways to evaluate the various courses needed for ISO certification. This resulted in a strategy that was mixed written tests, on-the-job structured observations, and proctored exam-lab combinations. Only courses that were truly part of the ISO strategy or were deemed job-critical were assessed at Level 2. By viewing the need for evaluation in this way, the company was better able to maintain the course learning assessments.

Case Example 2

Allied Health Associates, a midsized health care organization, wanted to provide an on-the-job coaching program that would assist in job transfer. WLP and the business managers determined jointly that some type of learning assessment needed to be in place postintervention. This assessment needed to be rigorous and needed to assess knowledge and skill, both before and following the intervention so that individual coaching plans could be designed. The coaching plans were to be specific and were to work at strengthening the skill and knowledge gaps that existed after the intervention.

WLP developed instruments, labs, and structured observations, as well as an objective on-the-job behavior worksheet to track what had changed as a result of the intervention and what would need reinforcement versus what would need knowledge or skill development. The coaching program has been in place for several years. Its popularity has grown and spread to other disciplines within the organization.

Case Example 3

Diversity was a key value of MarketMakers, a *Fortune* 100 company. It was important to this company that diversity be understood and embraced by every employee. The company defined *diversity* as "the acceptance and encouragement of differences in culture, thought, race, ideas, age, education, experience, ability or disability, creed, country, and beliefs." Because this was a core value, and one that it believed would influence current and future success, the organization asked its WLP department to create a diversity curriculum and to assess the difference the curriculum made in employees' embracing diversity practices.

WLP felt it needed to approach this Level 2 need differently. It designed a multifaceted learning assessment strategy that included an anchor-rated assessment to gauge feelings and how they changed, observation in a structured experience, and peer assessments of behaviors exhibited. It found that the curriculum made a difference in participants' beliefs and approaches to embracing and sponsoring diversity in their work groups and in their lives.

Is Level 2 Evaluation Needed?

The use of Level 2 evaluation varies from organization to organization. Level 2 can be a very valuable level of evaluation, and when used at the proper intensity, the effort expended can yield the desired information.

However, a Level 2 evaluation is not always needed. The questions used to determine Level 2 need are found in worksheet 5.1. Once you have answered yes or no to each of the questions, determine if those you have responded to with a yes are critical to your business objectives. If so, Level 2 evaluation will be useful, and the next step is to determine what intensity level is needed.

Worksheet 5.1: Questionnaire to Determine Level 2 Requirements

Yes	No	Level 2 Criterion Question
☐	☐	Are there certification or regulation requirements, or licensing criteria that create a need for learning assessment?
☐	☐	Does an employee need to perform this task to be competitive with other workers?
☐	☐	Have learning or performance requirements been well defined?
☐	☐	Have business partners requested some assurance that when participants have completed an intervention, they have increased their knowledge or skill level?
☐	☐	Is there a need for some form of assessment before an individual can advance to the next level of intervention (prerequisite)?
☐	☐	Are the consequences great if an individual is not able to understand or transfer the information in the intervention (e.g., safety issue, customer dissatisfaction)?
☐	☐	Is there a coaching or remedial program that is dependent on knowing what performance gaps exist postintervention?
☐	☐	Is it important to assess how effective this learning method was in comparison to others (e.g., OJT vs. classroom, Web-based training vs. OJT)?

Level 2 Measurement Intensity

Level 2 can be a powerful evaluation level at any intensity. Table 5.4 demonstrates that at even the lowest intensity, you can assess a learning change. At the low-intensity level you are estimating the learning change, and in the moderate- and high-intensity levels you are quantifying the learning change.

The information gained by implementing any of these three intensities can assist you in identifying remaining learning needs, potential ability to perform on the job, and potential flaws in the solution's design. Not only are there a variety of assessment tools that you can use to evaluate at Level 2 (table 5.2), but there are different methods for different purposes (such as a gain of skill versus a change in beliefs or confidence).

Building a Low-Intensity Tool

Level 2 low-intensity tools assess, without a great deal of time and effort, if a participant learned from the intervention. This does not necessarily mean that low-intensity tools won't take time or effort, but they require much less than moderate- or high-intensity tools. Even though low-intensity tools are much more subjective and perception based than moderate- or high-intensity tools, some degree of rigor is required in their development. For example, an unstructured observation that does not include performance standards or expected performance criteria is not appropriate for Level 2 evaluation; it is too subjective and perception based. To determine if learning has occurred, the observation script needs to provide

Table 5.4: Level 2 Evaluation Intensity Characteristics

Low-Intensity Characteristics	Moderate-Intensity Characteristics	High Intensity Characteristics
Test using behavior-anchored statements (subjective)	Structured tests that have been evaluated for reliability and viability	Structured tests that have been validated
Unstructured observations	Structured observation checklist completed by instructor, peer, other participant, or coach	Structured observation checklist completed by objective expert
Self-efficacy assessments that identify perceived learning change		

some guidance for the observer so the results can be measured.

Two of the three tools most commonly used for Level 2 low-intensity evaluations—self-efficacy assessments and tests using behavioral-anchored statements—are based on behavioral-anchored rating scales (BARS). This type of tool uses scales composed of "anchors." The anchors are descriptions of expected performance, typically grouped in sets of three, five, or seven. The first anchor statement describes the lowest expectation of performance. The next anchor builds on the first, and so on. Another way to view an anchor is to use it to establish what a person's performance is at a certain point in time and then use the anchor as a descriptive measuring device. For example, in the knowledge domain (as noted in table 5.3), a performance description would use the verbs that correspond with that level: recall, define, recognize, repeat, memorize, match, list, state, write, cite. In the comprehension domain the performance description would use that domain's corresponding list of verbs: translate, categorize, segregate, select, sort, discuss, recognize, identify, review, restate, interpret, classify, describe, distinguish, express, indicate, locate, tell, summarize. The anchor should contain three components:

1. *Performance definition:* This component describes what an employee does when demonstrating mastery of the knowledge or skill on the job. It is typically expressed as an activity or a behavior. For an employee who provides telephone support to customers, an example of a performance definition at the cognitive level of knowledge is "matches the customer's inquiry to the appropriate information screen from the customer service telephone system."

2. *Criterion:* This component describes the extent of performance to be considered acceptable. This part of an anchor is usually measurable. It is expressed in terms of quantity, quality, or cost. There are two kinds of criteria—process and product. Process criteria describe how well the task is to be performed. Examples of process criteria include the following:

   — following customer call protocol as described in the Call Service Guide

   — adhering to HAZCOM (hazard communications) safety practices as defined in the Safety Manual

   — completing a customer call within two minutes

   — having no more than three customers on call waiting.

Product criteria describe actions related to the product or task. Product criteria include

   — explains benefits and features of a product using the product guide

   — produces a network plan and manages it

   — recalls and states when the triage protocol is used and when it is not.

3. *Condition:* This component describes the conditions that must be in place for the performance to occur. Such conditions may include resources such as equipment, budget, or human resources that must be available for the employee to perform. Examples of condition descriptions are the following:

   — dependent on the availability of the SAP (Statistical Applications Program) accounting system (performance definition: identify customers' basic to complex needs given the context of the product strategy)

   — when a customer license begins with the original equipment manufacturer (performance definition: complete project phase 1 milestones within budget).

To develop a BARS instrument, you should write a minimum of three and up to nine anchors that each build on the one that precedes it. Tool 5.1 illustrates how to structure the BARS. First, identify the performance or learning objective that the intervention supports. Then in the grid below, develop each anchor by identifying the performance definition, criterion, and condition for each. Remember to build on each level of anchor (anchor 1 should be the lowest level of performance, anchor 2 at a higher level, and so on).

Tool 5.1: Example of How to Build Anchors

Performance or learning objective to be supported:

As a result of the learning experiences and performance support systems created by the WLP department, the sales force of PDQ Bank will be able to:

- Increase quota by recognizing prospect and customer needs and operational problems and matching the most appropriate product set to meet the need or overcome the problem.

Anchor	Cognitive Domain	Performance Definition	Criterion	Condition
1.	Knowledge	Matches the benefits and features of a new product to an existing customer	Using the approved operational problem and product solution matrix guide (product criterion)	When a customer has an operational problem that could be resolved by adding a product, such as overdraft protection for checking products
2.	Application	Explains the features and benefits of a product to a new customer	Using the product and competition online guide, by entering the competitor and type of product (product criterion)	When a customer asks how a product performs against a competitor
3.	Analysis	Probes for additional demographic information from a customer	Having no more than two customers in the waiting line (process criterion)	When a customer has a balance of over $10,000

Tool 5.2 illustrates how anchor statements are used to develop an assessment. As a pretest, supervisors rank their perception of their performance. As a posttest, they identify their performance as a result of the program.

Anchors can be difficult to create. Worksheet 5.2 is a tool that you may use individually or with a review group to validate the level (see table 5.2 linking Bloom's taxonomy to Level 2) of anchors in a supervisory assessment for objectivity and meaningfulness. Review each anchor against the criteria to ensure that it is written appropriately and meets the validation criterion. For any exceptions ("no" answers), determine how the statement could be restated so it is clearer, more related to the learning intent, or more usable to an employee,

instructor, manager, or peer completing the Level 2 evaluation using the BARS tool.

Self-efficacy assessments are another tool that can contain anchors at Level 2. You can use this type of assessment as a self-perception tool to measure confidence increase or a perceived belief change. This type of tool is useful in interventions such as sales training, management skill development, orientations, and awareness programs. Self-efficacy assessments can use anchors as a measure, or they can use a Likert scale, as demonstrated in tool 5.3.

Other types of Level 2 low-intensity evaluations include oral questions, which can be used to determine knowledge or comprehension acquisition, and

Tool 5.2: Example of an Assessment Based on Bloom's Domains

Objective: When given a customer problem, the employee uses the customer service telephone system to problem solve and report the information, or to determine if the problem needs to be escalated to a product technician.

Bloom's Cognitive Domain	Assessment Item
Domain 1: Knowledge	When provided with a customer's contract, an employee can determine which product licensing formula applies and calculate the potential fee the customer will be charged using the customer service telephone system.
Domain 2: Comprehension	An employee is able to define a customer's problem with a product and, using the customer service telephone system, describe the causal relationship among the product problem characteristics to a product technician.
Domain 3: Application	When provided with recent customer problem calls, product information, and marketing forecasts, the employee can design a potential new product schematic for the customer service telephone system.

Worksheet 5.2: Anchor Validation Criteria

Yes	No	Validation Criterion
☐	☐	Each anchor builds on the previous one (or is inclusive of the previous one).
☐	☐	Each anchor is concise.
☐	☐	The anchors do not include vague language such as "familiar with product terms" (better: "familiar with the features and benefits of the products") or "knows customers' needs" (better: "identifies customer needs using approved sales process").
☐	☐	The anchors do not include "laundry lists" such as needed equipment or resources.
☐	☐	Each anchor describes an observable or measurable behavior so that a manager or employee could objectively state, "Yes, I've done or seen that," or "No, I have not done or seen that."
☐	☐	The anchor is job relevant. It includes performance requirements that are specific to the job or competency as expected.
☐	☐	Each anchor includes an action verb related to the appropriate cognitive level.
☐	☐	The anchor clearly states the correlation between the skill or knowledge and the performance requirement.
☐	☐	The manager or employee is able to directly relate the anchor to the content of the intervention.

Tool 5.3: Self-Efficacy Assessment Using an Anchored Likert Scale

Directions: This self-assessment is to be completed after attending the financial management course. The purpose of this assessment is to rate your confidence in applying the knowledge, skills, and tools presented in this course **immediately after taking the course.**

Listed under each of the three categories in the assessment are statements related to the knowledge, skills, and tools that you should be able to apply to your work as a result of attending the class. Using the rating scale, indicate your confidence level in applying the knowledge, skills, or tools.

Once you have completed the assessment, indicate the topics for which you would like coaching assistance from your manager in the space provided below. This self-assessment will be given to your manager, who will conduct a follow-up meeting with you to discuss your confidence in applying the topics presented in the course. Because this is a self-assessment based on your perceptions, this assessment is not scored.

Application Category and Examples	1 Unsure of how to apply and will need help in doing so	2 Moderately unsure of how to apply and will need periodic guidance	3 Moderately confident of how to apply but may need assistance in doing so	4 Confident of how to apply and will be able do so independently	5 Extremely confident of how to apply and will be able to assist others in doing so
Knowledge (e.g., define concept of strategic cost management)					
Skills (e.g., analyze two vendors' financial approaches and determine which would most likely meet the organization's budget requirements)					
Tools (e.g., be able to use Excel comfortably)					

Application Category	Topics Requiring Coaching
Knowledge	1. _____
	2. _____
	3. _____
Skills	1. _____
	2. _____
	3. _____
Tools	1. _____
	2. _____
	3. _____

follow-up interviews, which can evaluate both learning and low-intensity transfer to the job (Level 3).

Building a Moderate-Intensity Tool

The data generated from moderate-intensity tools is more objective than that generated from a low-intensity tool. Of course, with the objectivity comes more effort and thought. Tests designed at Level 2 must be evaluated for reliability and viability.

- *Reliability* means that the test scores truly indicate takers' knowledge or skill. Only those with a higher knowledge or skill level will correctly complete the more difficult test items.

- *Viability* means that the test generates the type of response its developers intended. If analysis is being tested, then the test is structured to test analysis—for example, through exercises such

as simulations, word problems, case studies, and the like. True or false tests or other knowledge assessment tools will not have viability in assessing respondents' ability to analyze. Moderate-intensity tests at Level 2 should meet certain criteria that reinforce their reliability, viability, and other elements of good test design, as illustrated in table 5.5.

Testing needs to be well thought out, and some caution is suggested. Potential liability issues exist, and care needs to be taken with the following:

- use of test results to determine the potential qualification of an employee for hire or promotion

- use of test results to influence salary or pay adjustments

- testing when health or safety issues are present that require qualification or certification of employees to ensure they either understand the

Table 5.5: Criteria for Level 2 Moderate-Intensity Tests

Category	Test Criterion
Reliability	Are the test results similar for similar performers? Do high performers score high and low performers low? Do high performers miss the same types of items and low performers miss the same types of items, and are the two types different? When the responses to the test are tracked in several environments and occasions, are the results similar?
Viability	Does the test generate results that meet its purpose in testing? Do takers who pass the test demonstrate the ability associated with mastering the test? Do the items match the test objectives?
Validity	Does each objective have its own item? Is each test item related to specific intervention content? Can a direct connection be made between content and a test item? Do takers perform at the same level on validation test items? In other words, if you presented two math problems to test addition, would a taker who has mastered addition be likely to respond correctly to both? Do those being tested expect to be tested on the test's content? (For example, managers taking a budget class don't expect to be tested on performance evaluation techniques.) Have trick questions and techniques been avoided? Is the test fair?
Integrity	Would an expert reviewing the test be able to complete all test items? Do other individuals who write tests view the test items as acceptable and meeting the criteria? Do participants in the intervention who are tested view the test as "fair"? Are items free of ethnic, cultural, or gender bias?
Audit or predictive	Are employees who pass the test competent back on the job? Do others (e.g., managers, peers, customers) see expected knowledge or performance changes in those who are knowledgeable or skilled in the practice?

Category	Test Criterion
Edit	Is the item short? Wordy items may be confusing or misconstrued.
	Is only one question presented? Multiple questions (e.g., write the steps to the process and troubleshoot this process problem) should not be included in the same item.
	Does the item link directly to the intended objective?
Item answer	Are the item and the answer consistent with each other?
	Does each item have a compatible answer?
	Are answers written at the appropriate level and not misleading because of inappropriateness.
	Are "distractors," or wrong answers, absolutely incorrect?
	Are there no redundant answers?
	Is there enough information in the item to correlate with the correct answer?

safety issue or know what to do to prevent a health issue

• testing to prove compliance with specified environmental, government, safety, health regulation, or consensus standards.

When you use tests for these reasons, the following questions should be asked of the organization's attorneys:

1. Should the test's purpose be stated up front so there is no misunderstanding of intent?

2. What types of accommodations should be offered to disabled participants who wish to complete the test but are unable? (This is an issue whenever you give a test.)

3. What precautions can you take to ensure that the organization is not held responsible if results are used for hiring or promoting or if an employee is harassed in cases when testing was for other purposes, such as development or coaching?

4. How should test results be communicated so they are not misused?

Structured observations also are invaluable tools for a Level 2 moderate-intensity evaluation. They are particularly valuable if you will be measuring some degree of transfer to the job. It is very helpful to see the behavior demonstrated postintervention, but in a controlled environment, and then evaluate the same behavior back on the job. You can also obtain valuable job barrier information that can be used to modify interventions so the behavior is more likely to transfer. A structured observation provides linkage between what is learned and how it will be performed.

Tool 5.4 provides an example of a structured observation checklist. The purpose of this checklist is to help a peer, manager, instructor, expert, or coach conducting a structured observation to assess how effectively an employee is applying the specific steps or activities related to the key concepts in the course. Since this observation is being completed for performance improvement and coaching purposes, there is no scoring involved.

Observation checklists for Level 2 moderate- and high-intensity evaluations must be built on the objectives of the intervention. The observation checklist should provide the standards for performance so that the observer can consistently evaluate various employees using the same process and the same standards of evaluation. The difference between a moderate-intensity observation (as provided in tool 5.4) and a high-intensity observation is that the latter has a greater degree of rigor and spells out performance criteria for the observer. Worksheet 5.3 can assist you in developing an observation checklist.

Building a High-Intensity Tool

Both tests and structured observations are also used in Level 2 high-intensity evaluations. There are two main differences between moderate- and high-intensity testing. First, high-intensity tools must be validated and continually tracked for exceptions. Examples of exceptions include the following:

• High performers get lower scores on a test than low performers.

• Strong performers consistently score high regardless of culture, language, or other differences.

Tool 5.4: Structured Observation Sample Checklist

Directions: This structured observation checklist is to be completed during the observation as long as it does not interfere with the work of the person being observed or with the observation itself. Please complete the identifying information before the observation session.

Modules to be covered: _____

Date of observation: _____

Person being observed: _____

Person observing: _____

Part 1: Observation Form

The person being observed:	Acceptable	Needs Practice	Omitted
1. Is able to execute the steps outlined below in contracting with clients to negotiate cost reductions.			
Step 1: Identifies client need through client questionnaire	_____	_____	_____
Step 2: Determines client budget requirements	_____	_____	_____
Step 3: Identifies cost reduction requirements	_____	_____	_____
Step 4: Compares reduction requirements against customer contract	_____	_____	_____
Step 5: Finalizes customer cost agreement with Marketing Advisory Board	_____	_____	_____
2. Is able to resolve problems with customers using the customer service telephone system.			
Step 1: Probes customer using problem guide	_____	_____	_____
Step 2: Keys in product code	_____	_____	_____
Step 3: Identifies troubleshooting directions	_____	_____	_____
Step 4: Guides customer through problem resolution	_____	_____	_____
Step 5: Determines if problem is resolved	_____	_____	_____

Part 2: Need for Follow-Up

Activities Requiring Coaching	Potential Performance Improvement Actions
_____	_____
_____	_____
_____	_____

Worksheet 5.3: Observation Tool Development Checklist

Development Cue	Notes for a Specific Observation Tool
What will be observed, and why?	
How will it be observed?	
Where will the observation take place?	
When will it be observed?	
Will there be multiple areas of observation?	
Have the observation techniques been standardized and executed consistently across groups?	
Have the employees to be assessed or observed been notified?	
Have the employees involved been given an explanation of what will happen as a result of the observation?	
Are there performance standards that can be used?	
Has the scoring of the observation tool (e.g., anchoring, Likert scale, standards) been determined?	

- Those tested achieve similar scores when retested.

Typically, high-intensity tests are used for certification, safety, or performance assessment. Consequently, errors are much more costly because customers (or those being certified) will be dissatisfied if they don't know what they should. This affects brand, re-work, costs, and revenue generation. Errors on performance assessments can cause morale problems, retention problems, and even lawsuits.

Statistical analysis on each item should be completed, and it is recommended that you use a testing software package or identify an expert in statistical analysis for testing when using high-intensity testing. At the very least, chi-square analysis should be done to ensure that item performance is comparable test after test, and standard deviations should be calculated to determine variances between scores. Standard deviation, when calculated, will tell you the performance differences. Are the scores very close to each other, or are they shaped like a bell curve? A bell curve is defined by the average deviation of scores from the average score of the group. How the curve is skewed tells test designers how the population scored. A group of high performers should skew the tail to the left. If the tail of the curve is skewed to the right, it means most test takers performed low on the test, of concern because the test is probably poorly developed so the intervention will not work.

The second difference is that in high-intensity testing, an expert who can evaluate the skill or knowledge from a more technical point of view usually conducts observations. For example, expert observation would be required on a factory line, where a mistake may create scrap or cause an injury; the expert would evaluate the employee's ability to run the machinery postintervention. This is usually called a "certification." Special considerations for developing high-intensity tools are provided in table 5.6.

Table 5.6: Considerations in Developing High-Intensity Tools

Tool	Consideration
Testing	Deeper validation against testing criteria is necessary.
	Statistical analysis must be completed using standardized testing theory.
	Item inconsistencies should be tracked over time.
	Maintenance on tests is crucial.
	Legal risks need to be managed.
	Linkage to the content of the intervention is required.
	Assurance that the employee has the skills or knowledge to perform is necessary.
Observations	Training of experts on the how-tos of observation is critical.
	Ensuring that observation standards encourage consistency is crucial.
	Observation results must be tracked and compared statistically.
	The observation tools must be maintained so they are consistent with content and performance objectives.
	Use of observation feedback as a coaching device is an additional benefit.
	Linkage to Level 3 (Behavior/Transfer) observation is natural.

Chapter Summary

This chapter defined Level 2 (Learning) and presented criteria for when to use it. The varying types of learning assessments were identified, and the relationship of Bloom's taxonomy to Level 2 evaluation was discussed. How to build Level 2 tools of low, moderate, and high intensity was presented and examples of tools for each level of intensity provided. Additionally, the use of BARS in Level 2 tests and assessments was addressed.

Discussion Questions

The following questions are provided to help you apply what you learned in this chapter:

- What is Level 2 evaluation?

  _____

  _____

- When is a Level 2 evaluation needed?

  _____

  _____

- What type of learning information is needed in your organization?

  _____

  _____

- When would you use a Level 2 low-intensity tool?

  _____

  _____

- When would you use a Level 2 moderate-intensity tool?

  _____

  _____

- When would you use a Level 2 high-intensity tool?

  _____

  _____

- What is an anchor, and how does it relate to Level 2 evaluation?

  _____

  _____

Developing Level 3 (Behavior/Transfer) Tools

Was the intervention really useful? Are those who took part in the intervention actually using it back on the job? Are employees doing their jobs differently? These are the questions asked in Level 3 (Behavior/Transfer) evaluation.

Many WLP professionals balk at completing Level 3, because it is much more difficult to measure than other levels. So much is out of their control, especially since it is usually not possible to provide the "perfect" job environment where behavior change is supported and encouraged. But this objection is also clearly one of the benefits of evaluating at Level 3. A real understanding of the barriers that exist, which a well-developed Level 3 approach will provide, will help you articulate to your business partners the environmental or job changes that need to occur. The objections of "it's out of our control" or "it's not a perfect world" are exactly what the solution should address. Evaluating our effectiveness back on the job is really a step in the direction of evaluating our effectiveness in developing solutions.

For example, an HMO had many hiring and performance problems resulting from poor job interviews. As a result, the WLP department recommended an interview process that included interview questions, guides, and ranking tools based on behavioral interviewing. The supervisors initially complained that they were often forced to place candidates who were not qualified because of labor shortages or management replacement needs, so many asked, "How does this help me?" The new interview process provided the supervisors not only with interviewing tools but also with knowledge and skill gaps tools to assess which candidate was the most qualified and what type of performance gap existed so they could begin to close it. This on-the-job objection pointed out a hidden benefit from the design.

Some additional benefits you can realize from measuring the degree of transfer of knowledge, skills, and beliefs back to the job are

- identifying the barriers that prohibit or limit the amount of transfer to the job

- identifying what can promote transfer to the job so it can be duplicated in other areas
- identifying what other support or assistance is needed
- quantifying the time it actually takes to make the behavior change so it can be planned for and recognized.

In chapter 1 we discussed the importance of balancing viewpoints in evaluation. Balancing measures is equally important in Level 3 and 4 evaluations. Balancing measures enables you to provide a fuller picture not only of how the solution is performing, but also, when change occurs, how it is affecting the environment or solution. For example, if you evaluate a sales program and use only the measure "sales," you don't really know if the solution is causing the increase (and hopefully not the decrease) in sales or if it is an incentive, environmental, competition, or other type of issue. Having several different measures with different viewpoints gives you a fuller picture of the solution's impact, as can be seen in table 6.1. By having a more complete picture, you will be able to explain in more detail the impact of the solution. In other words, balanced measures provide a performance audit trail. You can say with confidence that participants are using what they learned, that they are faster at what they do, that they are having the desired performance results, and that the desired results are meeting the business objectives.

Balancing measures also has another advantage—it helps diagnose the impact of change. If a new product is launched, a sales incentive is changed, or competition increases, you can identify where the change occurs. Is it percentage of compliance with sales steps, is it time to proficiency, is it percentage of closed sales, is it profit per sale? You can then determine what needs to change and how to approach the change without reinventing the wheel.

Balancing measures is much more critical in Levels 3 and 4 because of the impact of the changes. For

Table 6.1: Level 3 Measurement Methods

Balanced Measure	What It Measures	Importance of This Measure in Balancing Measures
Percent of compliance with sales steps	Pre- and postsolution observation of an individual following sales steps (measures ability to do process back on the job)	This measure presents a picture of what individuals are doing on the job pre- and postintervention and how their behavior has changed. It also identifies where they are still having problems (such as in overcoming resistance or discussing the technical issues with a product). This measure provides information about whether they are using what they learned on the job.
Time to proficiency	Pre- and postsolution measure of how quickly an individual can adapt to the sales process (measures the learning that occurred in "job terms")	Typically measure is applied to newer employees as time to proficiency measures learning curve. It shows if the solution results in more competent employees. This measure indicates whether individuals are spending less time learning and increasing their sales aptitude as a result of the solution.
Percent of closed sales	Pre- and postsolution determination of no. of sales closed (measures productivity increase when compliance with process occurs)	This measure indicates whether, as a result of following the solution's guidelines, employees are able to close more sales.
Profit per sale	Pre- and postsolution assessment of profit per sale (measures revenue gain or loss)	This measure balances the percent of closed sales by showing if the sales are profitable. This measure helps answer the questions, Are individuals merely closing any sale, or is the sale being qualified and therefore profitable? This measure helps establish that individuals are making "quality" sales.

example, a large department store chain that prided itself on customer service reinforced the belief that "the customer was always right" by accepting any item a customer brought back with "no questions asked." As time went by, returns were cutting into profits.

Management decided that this "return behavior" had to change, so it instituted a new policy that any returns an employee accepted would cut into that employee's incentive pay. Oops! After this decision was made, employees accepted few returns, telling customers they could not return the item because the garments were worn or because they did not have a receipt. Suddenly dissatisfaction was high among both customers and employees—no big surprise.

Although the company had indeed changed the behavior and the cost of returns had lowered, a bigger and more costly problem was created. Consequently, the company changed back to the previous policy and incentive program but created return policies that were clearly outlined. After this, the cost of returns decreased, but without customer and employee backlash. This demonstrated clearly the necessity of balancing the viewpoints of all parties involved.

It is important to determine if skills and knowledge learned or presented in an intervention have been applied back on the job. After all, the behavior change is a means to an end, and the end is results. To help you build expertise in Level 3 evaluation, this chapter focuses on the following:

- defining Level 3 evaluation
- baselining current behavior
- case examples illustrating how Level 3 has been used
- determining if Level 3 is needed
- describing Level 3 measurement intensity
- building a Level 3 low-intensity tool
- building a Level 3 moderate-intensity tool
- building a Level 3 high-intensity tool.

Defining Level 3 Evaluation

Level 3 is all about determining what, if any, change has occurred in the way in which someone does his or her job as a result of the intervention. Thus, the key to measuring Level 3 outcomes is to identify beforehand what change is expected. This seems obvious, and expected changes should have been identified in the needs assessment or as part of the design of the intervention, but too often they are not. Not having identified expected behavior changes, or performance objectives, makes measuring at Level 3 virtually impossible. Worksheet 6.1 can assist you in linking the content of the intervention (regardless of media or delivery method) to the expected behavior change. The intent of this worksheet is to help you link the learning objectives for the intervention to the intervention's content, performance objectives, and current performance (or baseline).

At the top of the worksheet, enter the title of the intervention, or a description of the intervention's purpose if it does not have a title. In column 1, enter the identified learning objectives. In column 2, list the content of the intervention that corresponds to the learning objectives. In column 3, identify the performance objectives that should be met by someone who has successfully met the learning objectives. Finally, in column 4, enter the baseline performance of the population that will be affected by the intervention. A *baseline* is a set of data that defines what the situation is at a certain period of time (usually before the intervention) and that is compared with postimplementation results.

Baselining Current Behavior

Establishing a baseline is a fundamental task in conducting a Level 3 evaluation. It will be very hard for you to determine if the intervention was successful if there is no documentation of what the situation was prior to the intervention. Worksheet 6.2 is a baseline considerations checklist that can help you identify the main activities to consider when establishing a performance baseline for a Level 3 evaluation. Check off each consideration after it has been reviewed and dealt with.

Worksheet 6.3 is provided to help you establish and document a baseline. This is a two-part form. In part 1, first identify the measures that will be used (e.g., sales, errors, scrap), and enter each in the first column. Then complete the remaining five columns for each measure identified. In the second column, list the objectives that would build skills or knowledge that should affect the measure when used. In the third column, identify any on-the-job sources for baseline data. In the fourth column, list the intervention source that will be used. The fifth column identifies any tools that may need to be

---

Worksheet 6.1: Identifying Expected Behavior Changes

Intervention: Product knowledge orientation

Learning Objective	Intervention Content	Performance Objective	Current Performance
After the product knowledge orientation, the sales representatives will be able to recognize a customer need and match the need to the appropriate products' features and benefits.	Identifying customer cues Mastering products' features and benefits Identifying complementary products Defining operational problems and determining appropriate product mix to overcome	Increase in quota Increase in new product sales (%, no., and $) Increase in cross sales (no. and $)	Only 20% to 30% of sales force accurately identifies customer cues and responds with appropriate products. Operational problems are often not resolved because of inappropriate product "solution."

Worksheet 6.2: Baseline Consideration Checklist

❑ The measures (e.g., errors, defects, sales) have been identified.

❑ The learning objectives of the intervention being evaluated at Level 3 have been identified and linked to the measures.

❑ The baseline measures that will be used in conjunction with or as part of the intervention activities have been identified.

❑ The availability of the required baseline data (e.g., reports, statistics) has been confirmed.

❑ The issues or factors that could affect the measures, such as management change, reorganizations, or sales incentives, have been identified, and a plan for addressing these issues or factors has been developed and agreed to.

❑ The potential changes that will take place between the baseline and implementation have been identified, and a determination has been made whether the data needs to be normalized.

❑ Historical data and sources that exist for baseline measures have been identified and validated.

❑ The methods that will be used to measure improvement (e.g., rating scales, surveys, interviews, observations) have been identified.

❑ Baseline tools and postperformance intervention tools have been reviewed so that no gaps exist.

❑ If historical data such as reports and statistics does not exist for baseline measures, a plan and methods for gathering the data have been identified.

❑ Methods to compare and analyze baseline data against postintervention results (e.g., target outcome, baseline-postimplementation difference, performance outcome to goal) have been identified.

❑ The Baseline Documentation Worksheet (worksheet 6.3) has been completed.

❑ When and to whom to report the baseline results have been identified.

---

developed to gather data for the baseline, and the final column identifies any potential issues regarding the data that are known prior to measurement.

In part 2, document the results of the baseline measurement. In column 1, list the measures that were ultimately used for the baseline, and complete each of the remaining three columns for each measure. Column 2 identifies the sources that were used for the measure, including any sources that were used to validate the original data collected. Column 3 documents the results of the measurement data. Finally, column 4 documents any issues known regarding the baseline data.

When you have completed the baseline and defined the expected behavior postintervention, you should document this information in the Behavior Gap Analysis Worksheet (worksheet 6.4). This worksheet acts as an audit trail to document the expected behavior, the current behavior, and the "behavior gap" between the two. The behavior gap is identified from information that is known within the organization at this point, such as performance feedback, assess-

ments, or self-reports, and will be validated during the baseline. The worksheet then identifies how the intervention should close the gap. This ties the Level 3 evaluation back to the intervention.

Level 3 Measurement Approaches

One of the difficulties WLP professionals encounter in doing Level 3 evaluation is identifying which method can provide the appropriate information. Table 6.2 describes various methods that can provide Level 3 data.

The degree of intensity of the intervention often depends on the extent to which the intervention will be used. If a large population will use the intervention, often it is desirable to do some form of Level 3 evaluation. But even when only a few employees will use the intervention, the business need for the transfer can outweigh the effort and cost of measuring it. Measuring the transfer to the job does have one final benefit: Frequently what is measured is done, because knowing they'll be evaluated encourages people to change.

Worksheet 6.3: Baseline Documentation

Part 1: Documentation of Baseline Sources

Measure	Intervention's Related Enabling Objective	Employer Source for Baseline Data	Intervention Source for Baseline Data	Tools to Be Developed	Potential Baseline Data Concerns
Quota ($ and no.)	Resolving operational problems with appropriate product mix	Sales reports Call center reports	Observations	None needed	Observations may be biased

Part 2: Documentation of Baseline Results, Sources, and Issues

Measure	Source Used	Baseline Measure	Gaps, Inconsistencies, Concerns, and Normalization Issues
Quota	Sales reports Call center reports	Quota increased by 15%	Baseline of quota was completed in quarter 2 and intervention results were remeasured in quarter 4. Data needs to be normalized for timing comparison.

Case Examples

Case Example 1

Power Utilities had a high employee turnover rate across jobs. Investigation of the problem revealed that employees didn't feel tied to the company. Communication was poor, and there was little or no employee performance management or development. To break this cycle, the company initiated a supervisory course that emphasized teamwork, communication, and

"employee management." The program was costly, and senior management was concerned that it would not be effective and that good money would be spent on a poor solution.

To both reinforce the transfer and to ensure that it indeed was occurring, the WLP team built the program so managers had to work in peer groups preparing communication meetings for their employees and developing employee cross-training opportunities. Each supervisory team built its cross training and communication programs, and results were reported on a

Worksheet 6.4: Behavior Gap Analysis Worksheet

Expected Behavior	Current Behavior and Source	Behavior Gap and Source	How Intervention Should Close the Behavior Gap	Estimated % of Knowledge and Skill Transfer Postintervention
Sales representative is able to identify customer cues and resolve operational problems with correct product mixes.	Sales representatives currently miss many cues and recommend wrong solutions to problems or make no recommendation at all. (Sources: call center, needs assessment documentation)	Product knowledge and customer knowledge gaps (Source: needs assessment documentation)	Increase knowledge and application of customer and product matches	50%

Table 6.2: Level 3 Measurement Approaches

Method	Rationale	Description
Survey (Likert scale)	A low-intensity Level 3 approach that if developed for Level 2 can also be used at Level 3 and provide subjective data about transfer to the job.	A survey that uses a Likert scale (see chapter 5) to assess perceived transfer (e.g., tool 5.3).
Survey (anchored)	A low-intensity Level 3 approach that if developed for a Level 2 can also be used at Level 3 and provide subjective data about transfer to the job.	A survey built with BARS (see chapter 5) to assess the extent of the transfer.
Structured observation	If developed for Level 2 can also be used at Level 3. For Level 3 it often requires supervisor or peer training as well so that the observation can be rated appropriately or effectively.	An observation that identifies behaviors, actions, and the standard of performance expected (see chapter 5).
Focus group or interview with script	When information is needed to compare various situations and individuals and to identify barriers to performance, this approach is especially useful because you can probe deeper to gain understanding.	A scripted interview or focus group with managers or users of the intervention (see tool 6.2).

Method	Rationale	Description
Productivity measure	Most likely the best approach, especially if the measure is being tracked already. It typically supplies nonbiased data regarding performance change and can be tracked historically for normalization if needed.	A standard measure that is already available and can be used to indicate performance change (e.g., number of calls taken, length of calls, error rate, scrap, retention, customer complaints, sales).
Mystery shopping	Highly intensive, as researchers often need to be trained; provides a wealth of information about customer service, sales process, and use of tools and processes.	A structured program in which researchers pose as customers at banks, stores, or other customer-driven organizations and use a set of published standards to rate the performance of service or sales personnel.
Control group vs. intervention group	Very useful if you are implementing a solution in stages, because you can compare the first groups to receive the intervention with those who have not to identify the impact of the solution. This approach provides data that are less easily challenged.	The control group does not (at least initially) participate in the intervention, whereas the intervention group does. The two groups are compared to determine if the intervention resulted in change.
Existing systems	If existing systems that track performance or performance results exist, it is best to use them. It involves less re-work and uses something all are familiar with.	There may be an existing system that traps performance data and provides information regarding change. For example, a system may provide information about the length of time it takes to resolve a technical problem. Another example would be a pre-existing multirater 360 feedback system.
Peer coaching	More intensive and highly dependent on the work environment, but it can be very useful as the evaluator coaches someone doing the same job. Most typically used with evaluation of new hires or high-potential employees. Combines evaluation with OJT.	Using structured coaching tools, peers work together at designated times to provide feedback and coaching and to ensure that transfer to the job is occurring.
Performance diary	When a picture is needed of what is actually happening on the job, this approach is very helpful. It can track interruptions, barriers, number of system problems, and other things that influence on-the-job performance. This approach is also very important as a follow-up to another approach if data are reported that point to a lot of undefined job barriers. The diary usually helps the evaluator determine the core problem by providing a record of the job as the employee sees it.	A performance diary is used to track an individual's actions to determine what change occurs and how. It is often cited as reinforcement for transfer to the job because it highlights unnecessary or nonproductive actions. In a performance diary the employee logs time spent on phone calls, number and type of interruptions, meetings, and so forth. It can also be used to track specific behaviors (e.g., sales process during sales calls).
Special assignment or project	If job duties do not necessarily lead to a demonstration of new knowledge or skills and behavior transfer is desired, often an assigned project (especially with a team made up of solution graduates) can be used to determine that the skills are transferrable and provide the desired results.	A special assignment or project is assigned to assist in the transfer of skills and knowledge and provide an immediate need to practice and transfer the skills. Typically there is some type of review as a part of the project to provide feedback and measure the transfer.

quarterly basis to senior management. In addition, an employee satisfaction survey was completed twice a year to monitor change. After the program's first year, more than 75 percent of the supervisors had completed the training and implemented the programs. The transfer results were outstanding—95 percent of the supervisors applied what had been learned back on the job, and as a result employee satisfaction increased by 15 percentage points.

Case Example 2

Merit Manufacturers had several assembly lines. To train the operators of these lines, the organization developed one-on-one on-the-job training sessions. Although the population to be trained was small, transfer to the job was a business need of the utmost importance both to promote the safety of the employees and to ensure that the products manufactured were error free and of high quality. A structured observation with set steps and standards for each step was completed at the end of the training, two days following the training, and during spot checks every two weeks. The results were positive. Not only did transfer occur in 100 percent of the employees, but it was also found that scrap, re-work, and supervisory interruptions decreased.

Case Example 3

Sunset Financial, located throughout the western United States, implemented a new computer system. The purpose of the system was to help customer service representatives increase closed sales and cross sales. The system and its online training were considered a packaged intervention. By the time it was implemented companywide, the cost of the combined intervention was over $10 million. Senior management requested evaluation of both transfer to the job and return-on-investment (ROI) from the WLP and information systems departments.

Unfortunately, after initiating the transfer measures, WLP found that transfer was very low because of significant system problems. The system frequently timed-out during a customer transaction, increasing the time spent with a customer by 150 percent. Customer service representatives were not using the system, and their morale was very low because they believed that the money spent on the system could have been used much more productively.

Is Level 3 Evaluation Needed?

The three case examples make it clear that many different methods can be used to measure transfer to the job. However, you must be prepared for bad news or negative results when doing a Level 3 evaluation, because barriers to transfer back on the job do occur. Learning to identify barriers and determining if they

can be overcome is a significant benefit of implementing Level 3 evaluation.

So when is it appropriate for you to engage in a Level 3 evaluation? You can use the tool in worksheet 6.5 when discussing if Level 3 evaluation should be included as part of your evaluation strategy. Review each of the criteria and enter "yes" or "no" in column 1 for each item. The more yes responses you record, the greater the need for a Level 3 component in your evaluation strategy.

Level 3 Measurement Intensity

Level 3 probably has the greatest range of methods and tools of all of Kirkpatrick's levels of evaluation. Consequently, you will need to carefully consider the business need and purpose to determine the intensity of effort that should be expended. Even the lowest level of intensity will be time consuming but will afford valuable information and should be considered (table 6.3).

Building a Low-Intensity Tool

To conduct a low-intensity Level 3 evaluation, the following must occur:

1. The performance objectives must be linked to the learning objectives, the content, and a baseline; alternatively, a control group should be conducted.

2. The performance objectives become the core of the low-intensity instrument and are formed into statements or questions. Tool 6.1 provides an example of this type of tool.

3. The data gathered from the Behavior Gap Analysis Worksheet (worksheet 6.4) are compared with the data collected from tool 6.1 and the percentage of transfer assessed.

Building a Moderate-Intensity Tool

The key difference between a moderate-intensity and a low-intensity Level 3 tool is that the standards of performance for the moderate-intensity tool are more detailed and leave little room for interpretation. The process for ensuring that your tool meets these two criteria is as follows:

Worksheet 6.5: Level 3 Criteria

Yes	No	Level 3 Evaluation Criterion
☐	☐	Will the intervention affect key business drivers?
☐	☐	Will the intervention be costly or perceived as costly?
☐	☐	Does the intervention have high visibility?
☐	☐	Is the intervention the first time a new media or performance model will be used?
☐	☐	Is it critical that the behaviors resulting from the intervention be transferred to the job?
☐	☐	Is it important to track barriers to transferring the behaviors, skills, or knowledge?
☐	☐	Is there customer demand for the skill or knowledge that should be transferred to the job?
☐	☐	Will the intervention support a key change, management principle, or strategy that is critical to the organization as a business?
☐	☐	Have other interventions failed in the past or has behavior not been sustained, and is it important to determine if and why this happens again?
☐	☐	Will there be a large population involved?
☐	☐	Will the intervention be based on the business results it will provide?
☐	☐	Has management requested or is it interested in determining if what has been learned through the intervention is actually being used?

Table 6.3: Level 3 Evaluation Intensity Characteristics

Low-Intensity Characteristics	Moderate-Intensity Characteristics	High-Intensity Characteristics
Follow-up surveys with undefined Likert scale, open-ended questions that allow for interpretation	Anchored survey statements (leave little to no room for interpretation) Structured observation checklist (completed by manager or coach) Focus groups with structured scripts Interviews with structured scripts	Productivity or individual performance metrics (number of closed sales, call wait times, re-work statistics, return customers) Mystery shopping Structured observation checklist (completed by objective expert)

1. The performance objectives must be linked to the learning objectives and content and a baseline conducted or control group identified.

2. The performance objectives become the core of the instrument and are formed into statements or questions.

3. Standards for each performance objective are identified and become the criteria for the Level 3 tool.

4. Using the data gathered from the Behavior Gap Analysis Worksheet (worksheet 6.4), the data collected from the new tool is compared and the percentage of transfer assessed.

Tool 6.1: Low-Intensity Level 3 Tool Example

Manager Follow-Up Survey
(INSERT TITLE OF SOLUTION HERE)

Your employee(s) recently completed (INSERT NAME OF SOLUTION HERE). We are sending this follow-up survey to all of the participants' managers to collect information about the effectiveness of the program. A short series of questions follows regarding the performance of the employee(s) and any business change that may have resulted from the program.

If you had more than one employee attend this training intervention, you may either fill out one per employee or aggregate your answers and note any specific comments. If this survey is for more than one employee, please note the number of employees this survey represents.

Thank you very much for your support. If you have any questions about the training intervention or this survey, please feel free to contact me.

(INSERT NAME OF CONTACT HERE)

Number of employees this survey represents: _____

1. The following is a list of the concepts introduced in this class. Please check each one you feel your employee is beginning to apply.

    (INSERT THE KEY LEARNING OBJECTIVES FOR THE SOLUTION HERE)

2. Do you feel the employee has more confidence in (INSERT THE NAME OF SOLUTION OR A SHORT DESCRIPTION OF THE PURPOSE OF THE SOLUTION HERE)? (Check only one.)

    ____Marked increase   ____No change

    ____Slight increase   ____No opportunity to demonstrate new skills to date

3. How will you monitor the change in behavior or skill level? (Check all that apply.)

    ____Performance evaluation

    ____Business fundamental metric

    ____Status reports

    ____Informal one-on-one discussions

    Is there a specific measure you will use? (Please identify measures below.)

    _____

    _____

    _____

4. Can you identify any barriers that may prevent your employee from applying the knowledge, skills, or tools gained from this program?

5. Based on your observations of the knowledge and skills gained (or not gained) by the employee you sent, would you send additional employees with the same performance need to this program? ____Yes ____No

   Why or why not?

   _____

   _____

   _____

6. What do you think is the percentage of performance change as a result of this program?

   ____5% ____6-10% ____11-20% ____Greater than 20%

7. Is any follow-up needed with the employee by (INSERT YOUR COMPANY'S OR DEPARTMENT'S NAME HERE) to meet the expected performance requirements?

   _____

   _____

   _____

Thank you for your support and participation in our survey!

The Level 3 Evaluation Item Development Worksheet in worksheet 6.6 provides a structure for you to use when developing moderate-intensity tools. In column 1, list the performance objective for the intervention. In column 2, identify and specify what the expected performance will be postintervention; and in column 3, specifically state the standard or performance criteria that the expected performance should meet. For example, if the performance objective is to orient new employees within one week to the company's values, expectations, customers, and products and the expected performance is for a manager to meet with an employee within the first week on the job, then the performance standard is that employees will rate their orientation as acceptable and that their managers used the company handbook in a one-on-one session with them during the first week of employment.

You can use several of the tools provided in chapter 5 (or the premise for the development can be used), including BARS surveys and structured observations, in developing Level 3 tools. Another tool you may find valuable for moderate-intensity Level 3 evaluation is a structured interview or focus group. Tool 6.2 is an example of a structured interview tool.

Building a High-Intensity Tool

A high-intensity tool links the transfer of the intervention's skill or knowledge development back to the job with actual results. A high-intensity Level 3 evaluation determines if the intent of the intervention was applied back on the job and if it resulted in business indicator change as expected.

The measurement of Level 3 at a high intensity is more focused on the specifics of what is happening back on the job and, as a result, what is happening to the business. Consequently, such evaluation focuses on what are known as *leading indicators,* or expected behaviors and performance objectives, and *lagging indicators,* or business results. Leading and lagging indicators are coined as such because the leading indicator (behavior) occurs first and the lagging indictor (result) comes later. Worksheet 6.7 is a tool you can use to document the relationship between the two. Identify the measures that apply to the intervention in column 1 and the leading and lagging indicators linked to each measure in the remaining two columns. Leading indicators are what needs to happen if the

---

Worksheet 6.6: Level 3 Evaluation Item Development Worksheet

Performance Objective	Expected Performance	Performance Standard or Criterion
To increase sales of new and existing products (from approved listing) and increase sales representatives' quota according to business plan.	Sales representatives will use the product and customer information provided in conjunction with methods and processes demonstrated in the sales curriculum.	Products will be explained by features and benefits. Products recommended to customers and prospects will be from approved listings. Quota will increase in both number and dollars for sales representatives according to business plan.

Tool 6.2: Example of a Structured Interview Tool

Interview Question	Expected Result	Evidence of Performance
Tell me about a time in the past three months when you have used the Behavioral Interviewing questionnaire and skills that were provided to you in the Interviewing Workshop.	Use of packet at least once and most likely three to five times in the past month with new hires from outside of the company	Speaks to specific questions (may need to ask what questions were used) Discusses the results of the interview
What barriers have you encountered in using the Behavioral Interviewing questionnaire and skills during the past three months?	Most likely had some time constraints; interviews take longer using behavioral interviewing. May have had difficulty in using rating sheet. May have been uncomfortable in introducing process to interviewee	Lists actual barriers such as time, confidence, difficulty in using components of questionnaire kit. Discusses how he or she plans to overcome barriers

---

performance measure (e.g., number of sales made) is to be achieved, and lagging indicators measure end results (e.g., ROI and profit margin).

Worksheet 6.8 provides a checklist to gauge the reliability of the indicators. Using it will ensure that the leading and lagging indicators you have identified and

linked to the measures are reliable and will measure what is needed for evaluating at Level 3. You can use this worksheet in discussions of the indicators after completing worksheet 6.7.

Finally, an example of a high-intensity tool is provided in tool 6.3. This tool is a performance diary that participants are to use postintervention in a Level 3 evaluation. Participants are instructed to document in the diary the actions they take on the job that should reflect an increase in knowledge and skills for each of the job measures and performance expectations addressed through the intervention.

Just because an employee transfers the knowledge and skills learned through an intervention to the job does not guarantee a gain in expected business results. One can transfer the intervention yet achieve the "wrong" results (e.g., an employee might close more sales, but the sales aren't qualified and so are not profitable). Balanced measures provide you with more information that helps you see the total picture, and that is why a balanced approach is particularly important when you conduct a Level 3 or Level 4 evaluation.

Worksheet 6.7: Documenting Leading and Lagging Indicators

Intervention: Introduction to sales process

Measure	Leading Indicator	Lagging Indicator
Quota (No. and $)	Sales representatives act on customer cues and recommend appropriate products.	Increase in sales profits

---

Worksheet 6.8: Leading and Lagging Indicators Reliability Checklist

Yes	No	Reliability Factor
☐	☐	Does the indicator reflect program objectives?
☐	☐	Does top management value the indicator?
☐	☐	Can the indicator be computed for specific employees?
☐	☐	Is the output from the indicator available on a timely basis?
☐	☐	Can enough data be collected for reliable measurement?
☐	☐	Is the indicator free from known bias?
☐	☐	Does the indicator take into consideration individual confidentiality?
☐	☐	Is the indicator stable?
☐	☐	Is the indicator consistent?
☐	☐	Is the degree of accuracy suitable for the purpose?

Tool 6.3: Performance Diary Form

Intervention:

Measure(s):

Performance Expectation(s):

Performance Objective(s):

Action or Behavior	Date	Equipment or Tools Used	Environment	Duration	Results

Chapter Summary

This chapter defined Level 3 (Behavior/Transfer) evaluation and identified the conditions under which it would be conducted. The importance of baselining was presented, as were many methods to use to conduct Level 3 evaluations. Also included in this chapter was discussion of how to build Level 3 tools at low, moderate, and high intensity, along with example of tools at each level.

Discussion Questions

The following questions are provided to help you apply what you have learned in this chapter:

• What is Level 3 evaluation?

_____

_____

• When is Level 3 evaluation needed?

_____

_____

- How is balancing the measures important to Level 3 evaluation?

  _____

  _____

- What type of Behavior/Transfer information is needed in your organization?

  _____

  _____

- What is baselining, and what is its importance in Level 3?

  _____

  _____

- When would you use a low-intensity Level 3 tool?

  _____

  _____

- When would you use a moderate-intensity Level 3 tool?

  _____

  _____

- What is a leading indicator?

  _____

  _____

- What is a lagging indicator?

  _____

  _____

  _____

- When would you use a high-intensity Level 3 tool?

  _____

  _____

Developing Level 4 (Results) Tools

*T*he 2000 *ASTD State of the Industry Report* (ASTD, 2000) stated that 9 percent of Training Investment Leaders and only 3 percent of the ASTD Benchmarking Forum participants actually conducted Level 4 (Results) evaluations. This represented a slight increase over the previous year. The low use of Level 4 evaluation is indicative of the difficulty inherent in this level of evaluation. Conducting a Level 4 evaluation is difficult because

- it is expensive in resources and time
- results are hard to isolate to a specific intervention
- results typically occur over a longer period of time: Level 4 cannot be completed in 30, 60, or even 90 days.

That said, there are still significant benefits in conducting a Level 4 evaluation. Evaluation at this level forces you to step back to gain perspective on the big picture. The fact is that other things influence the results, and sometimes you should take all the factors into consideration. This does not detract from the evaluation; rather, it strengthens the information provided to management to help them make key decisions.

For example, if Level 4 evaluation reveals that sales dip when new competition hits, but that with incentives and a focus on enhanced sales skills you can overcome some of the "new player syndrome" (when the competition is seen as better because it's new and unknown), the business overall is helped. Evaluation at Level 4 also provides WLP with important business information such as how satisfied customers are, how changing a certain behavior influences results, and how interventions can be designed differently to have a greater impact. Conducting a Level 4 evaluation creates a partnership between business managers and WLP.

The following topics related to Level 4 evaluation are included in this chapter:

- defining Level 4 evaluation
- case examples illustrating how Level 4 has been used
- determining if Level 4 is needed
- describing Level 4 measurement intensity
- building a Level 4 low-intensity tool
- building a Level 4 moderate-intensity tool
- building a Level 4 high-intensity tool
- determining return-on-investment (ROI).

Defining Level 4 Evaluation

Level 4 evaluation provides information about how the intervention actually changed the business environment and influenced certain outcomes. Some leaders in evaluation separate Level 4 into two levels: Level 4 as business results and Level 5 as ROI. For the purposes of this chapter, Level 4 includes both. In the book *The Balanced Scorecard,* Kaplan and Norton (1996) presented a strong case that financial indicators (like ROI) are important but provide a "rear-view mirror" picture of what is happening. A change in retention figures is seen long before it is reflected in the cost of labor. Therefore, financial indicators should be only one part of what you look for in a Level 4 evaluation.

One of the benefits of using both a business result and a financial indicator (like retention and cost of labor) is that you can determine that, for example, an improvement in retention led to a reduction in the cost of labor. After conducting a Level 4 evaluation, you would know if retention really had played a significant part in the cost of labor. This is important data when designing large and expensive programs or when determining if an expensive companywide intervention should be implemented.

Level 4 evaluation should be part of an evaluation strategy when tangible results are part of the products, services, and interventions provided by WLP. The information sought in a Level 4 evaluation should determine business results and financial indicators—for example,

- reduction of scrap
- decrease in time to proficiency
- decrease in errors
- decrease in customer complaints
- increase in sales or cross-sales
- improvement in customer perception
- decrease in product customization
- decrease in return calls
- return-on-investment, return-on-equity, or return-on-assets
- decrease in days of inventory
- decrease in current liabilities to equity.

Evaluation at this level relates the results of the intervention to business improvements. Often it is these results that were the very reason for implementing a program. Level 4 evaluation helps you tie what was expected to what was realized and provides important information about whether or not the strategy or intervention was on track. Level 4 evaluation should provide closure on a full-circle approach; you start with the business need and end up by quantifying the impact of

the solution on the business need. Table 7.1 demonstrates this by defining the business need and what will need to be quantified at the end.

Business conditions, including the business environment or state of the business, typically are discovered when you begin asking questions similar to those presented in table 7.1. Identifying these conditions helps identify the business value and can lead to determining measures. For example, if business conditions include a slow economy, a reduction in sales, and low turnover in inventory, then the value may be in identifying cost reductions or perhaps in introducing new products or product enhancements to attract sales. The related indicators would then be costs or new product innovation and time to market. This is further demonstrated in table 7.2.

Defining business conditions, values, and indicators facilitates the discussion of parameters. For example, if a business condition is a lack of software engineers and the business need is to generate new products using software engineers, then the value is in identifying high-potential employees who can replace the software engineers in product development. By presenting the information in this manner, senior management will usually be more willing to provide information about cost limitations, strategy impact, business plans, and competition, because they believe you have an understanding of the business issues.

Table 7.1: Preassessment for Level 4 Evaluation

Question Asked in Assessment	Question Answered in Evaluation Level 4
What is the business need?	Was the business need met as desired?
What are the specific outcomes desired?	Were the specific outcomes realized?
What benefits should be involved in providing this service, product, or intervention?	What were the benefits in providing this service, product, or intervention?
What is the most effective way to meet the need?	Was this the most effective way to meet the need?
How do we know (what is the evidence) that this need exists?	What is the evidence that the need was remedied by the intervention or strategy?
What are the objectives?	Were the objectives met?

Table 7.2: Identifying Performance (Result) Indicators

Business Condition	Business Value	Performance Indicator
High turnover	Reduce time employees need to become competent	Time to proficiency
High error rate	Make correct information accessible	Reduced errors
Customer dissatisfaction	Answer customers' questions consistently	Customer retention
Technology advances	Use technology tools appropriately	Productivity increase
Lack of cross sales	Make complementary product information available quickly	Increase in sales
Transaction completed too slowly	Make information available and easy to find	Increase in number of transactions
Reference material goes out of date quickly	Change reference material to just-in-time	Increase in consistent information Reduced errors
Volume out of capacity	Provide individual tools to handle higher volume	Increase in customer retention Increase in individual productivity rate

Case Examples

Case Example 1

Consolidated Financial Group implemented a comprehensive management development program. The program included multirater 360 feedback, identification of developmental needs, customized training plans, and alternative performance development such as special projects, job sharing, and the like. The program's primary goals were to cultivate future leadership among its employees, improve employee satisfaction, decrease turnover, and increase employee productivity and decision making.

The program was piloted with 15 managers. Because the program was expected to be expensive, it was piloted in Operations before implementation division-wide. The results of the pilot were very positive. All 15 managers completed the program. Ten received a promotion within eight months, and all of those promoted identified the training program as a strong contribution to their performance and promotion.

In addition, the managers as a group reported a 15 percent increase in employee satisfaction. All had some reduction in turnover in their immediate group. Employee productivity and decision making also improved in the groups of most of the managers who participated in the development program.

As a result of the positive results from the pilot program, the institution implemented the program across divisions, and, for most, the results were consistent with the pilot. A few departments even exceeded the pilot results.

Case Example 2

Interstate Insurance Company implemented an electronic performance support system (EPSS) in its call centers. The purpose of the system was to enable customer call employees to respond to customer questions and inquiries about product features and to basic questions about processes and procedures.

After installation of the system, the feedback from the call centers was so positive that the company began to consider expanding the EPSS to include other types of customer information. A Level 4 evaluation study determined that the EPSS had contributed to the following:

- decreased time to proficiency. New hires were able to answer calls independently and accurately in almost 60 percent less time than their predecessors.

- decreased supervisory time. As a result of the EPSS, supervisors found that they spent two to three fewer hours in problem escalation and answering questions for call center employees. The information and ease of use provided by the EPSS supported the employees in working more independently.

- decreased underwriting department time. The underwriting department found that the time it spent providing telephone support, explaining general processes and procedures, and responding to customer inquiries was reduced by 30 percent once the call center employees became fluent with the EPSS. As a result, the department was able to handle much of its backlog of work without hiring temporary employees and did not replace two workers when they transferred out of the department.

- cost-effectiveness. Financially, it was determined that the EPSS system would pay for itself within 18 months.

The results persuaded management to proceed with a phase 2 implementation of the EPSS system.

Case Example 3

E-biz, a technology company that offers certification for its programs worldwide, wanted to offer its reseller population a vehicle to provide training and support using wireless technology. They wanted the resellers to be able to access files, slides, email, and limited computer-based or Web-based training and to have access to instructor-led training files globally. In response to this need, the company began to use its own technology, which was a wireless PC.

The financial results were astounding. The previous cost per reseller was over $1,000 per node; the new wireless approach cost a little less than $200 per node. The one drawback was that large files containing huge amounts of graphics were very slow to download.

The other saving was that written testing for certification could be set up anywhere there was a need (e.g., hotel rooms, extra office space) without the expense of rewiring the building or rerouting servers. The company received a return-on-investment for its new strategy, met a significant business need, and demonstrated their technology leadership.

Is Level 4 Evaluation Needed?

If management already believes the intervention to be of value to the organization and is comfortable with other types of evaluation such as a Level 2 or 3, it may be prudent to move more slowly with a Level 4 evaluation because of its higher cost in finances and time.

The Level 4 criteria listed in worksheet 7.1 may be useful to you in determining what role Level 4 evaluation can play in an organizational or for an intervention evaluation strategy. Review each of the criteria and enter yes or no in column 1 for each item. The more yes responses, the greater the need for a Level 4 component in the evaluation strategy.

Level 4 Measurement Intensity

You will need to link Level 4 evaluation fairly closely to business measures or financial indicators; consequently, Level 4 has the fewest tools, regardless of intensity (table 7.3).

Building a Low-Intensity Tool

Although most WLP products, services, and interventions are created and implemented with results in mind, identifying evidence that there has been a change is not always worth the effort. And unless the results are clear, it may be better for you to begin with a low-intensity tool to gain information about potential results and then graduate to the other tools. Interestingly, the type of information gained from a Results Expectations Survey (tool 7.1) frequently is acceptable to most parties, so the time and expense associated with other tools aren't necessary. If a Results Expectations Survey is included in the evaluation strategy approaches, the following information will be necessary:

- What are the business results?

- How do the performance objectives link to the business results (e.g., an increase in sales should increase departmental revenue)?

- How would an employee know if he or she was influencing the results?

- Who is it best to report to if there have been business results because of the intervention (manager, employee, other, all of the parties)?

- How might results information be validated?

The Results Expectations Survey is a tool that combines Level 3 and 4. It determines if the participant is using the intervention postintervention and, if so, what the results have been. Obviously, the weakness in this tool is its subjectivity; the subjective information can be validated through other, more intense tools.

Worksheet 7.1: Level 4 Criteria

Yes	No	Level 4 Criterion
☐	☐	Are the original goals, performance needs, and results tangible and easily linked to measures?
☐	☐	Is there a strong need to determine the business impact or determine if key indicators were influenced by the intervention for future decision making?
☐	☐	Is it important to determine if the intervention will pay (or has paid) for itself prior to becoming obsolete?
☐	☐	Is it important to determine what (if any) financial impact occurred?
☐	☐	If customer ROI was determined, would it be of value in marketing, business planning, or for other purposes?
☐	☐	Does pricing need to be determined?
☐	☐	Is the intervention critical to the organization and will the results be valued by the organization, therefore justifying the time needed to assess the return and results?
☐	☐	Is it important to the individual or the organization to determine whether there was specific impact on a business indicator?
☐	☐	Is it of importance to WLP's ongoing services and placement in the organization to track WLP's business alignment and report on it?
☐	☐	Was the implementation very expensive and does value need to be determined as a sound business practice?
☐	☐	Is it important to see what skills or knowledge being taught have the biggest payoff in results?
☐	☐	Is the program some sort of pilot (new program, new media, new delivery method), and is it important to determine what the results were and if the value was worth the expense?

Building a Moderate-Intensity Tool

Moderate- and high-intensity tools are less subjective than low-intensity tools. The key difference between a moderate-intensity tool and a high-intensity tool is that the former accepts (and even identifies if possible) other factors that may have caused or detracted from the results. A high-intensity Level 4 evaluation normalizes the data or reports the data on an individual basis so that it can be compared and analyzed thoroughly to determine the impact of the intervention separate from other results. For example, a management program with the purpose of increasing retention by identifying better candidate matches through behavioral interviewing is being evaluated at Level 4 moderate intensity. The retention results would indicate that it was both the training and the new stock incentives offered to employees with

Table 7.3: Level 4 Evaluation Intensity Characteristics

Low-Intensity Characteristics	Moderate-Intensity Characteristics	High-Intensity Characteristics
Follow-up surveys of approximate impact on business or financial indicators identified	Business or financial measures without separation of training or historic factors	Normalized business or financial measures Business and financial measures reported on an individual basis

Tool 7.1: Results Expectations Survey

You recently attended the Behavioral Interviewing course. This survey is designed to enable you to describe your experiences in transferring the intervention to the job and to identify the outcomes. Your assistance in completing this survey is greatly appreciated.

1. How many interviews have you participated in during the six months since you finished the program?

   ____1-5   ____6-10   ____10-25   ____More   ____None

2. Of the interviews you participated in, in what percentage did you use your Behavioral Interviewing tool kit?

   ____0%   ____1-10%   ____11-50%   ____51-75%   ____76-100%

3. If you used your Behavioral Interviewing tool kit, describe how you used the tools in the kit.

4. How did your Behavioral Interviewing course and kit assist in or detract from the task of interviewing?

If you have used the Behavioral Interviewing course and kit, please answer the questions below by placing a checkmark in the box that corresponds with your response. (If you have not used the content from the course or kit, please do not complete the information below.)

As a result of the course or kit, I am now able to:	Much More Easily	More Easily	With the Same Effort	With More Difficulty	With Much More Difficulty
Analyze the fit between the individual and the position and the culture					
Use past experience to predict future performance					
Use a standard set of criteria to determine an individual's capabilities					
Document an interview					
Rate an interviewee against another with objective feedback					
Use documented performance requirements to develop behavioral interviewing questions					
Control the interview to gain the information I need to make a decision					
Reduce the time it takes to write an interview script					
Create an atmosphere to discuss candidate strengths and weaknesses					

If you used the content from the course or kit, what outcomes do you think were influenced? Explain in as much detail as possible why you think this is so. (If an outcome was not influenced by the course or kit, please write "no" next to that outcome.)

Outcome	Explanation of Impact
Time to prepare for interviewing:	
Securing the right candidate:	
Retention:	
Time to proficiency:	
Cost of labor:	
Turnover:	
Respect for organization (organizational public perception):	
Decreased training time:	
Decreased coaching time:	
Other (please be as specific as possible):	

the company longer than 18 months that improved retention, and not changes in the economy.

WLP interventions usually combine with other factors to contribute to the desired business results. Moderate-intensity evaluation recognizes the other factors and states that these things all played a part in the results.

One of the reasons WLP professionals give for not engaging in a Level 4 evaluation is the difficulty in measuring results or getting to the data. Surprisingly, in most cases, the data is there, and it is just a matter of figuring out who has it. Table 7.4 lists common measures that can help you determine intervention effectiveness.

If the data is already being collected, the chances of determining the results increase because less effort needs to be put into getting it. In addition,

1. The time and expense are less than when you have to develop the measures for the intervention alone.

2. Historic data usually are available that allow you to monitor the effect of other factors besides the intervention.

3. If preintervention measurement data was not collected, it may be available from other sources to provide a baseline comparison.

4. Using existing measures solidifies the linkage of the intervention to the business and enhances the business partnership.

When you complete a Level 4 evaluation at a moderate or high intensity, the primary goals should be to use the information gathered from the evaluation to

1. improve the intervention

2. make better decisions regarding WLP products and services

3. promote business relationships and satisfaction across the organization.

Table 7.4: Typical Business Measures

Type of Measure	Potential Measure	Linkage to Intervention
Operations	Project profitability Price-earnings ratio Asset utilization ratio Revenue per employee Unit costs Indirect expenses Scrap Errors Work to re-work ratio Quality indicators Service statistics Time to delivery Cycle time Service guarantees Returns Defect-free products or parts Value for money Warranty claims Availability of service or product Audit quality Sourcing and distribution	Has planning or production improved because of the intervention?
Productivity	Time to proficiency Product production No. of customers served or calls answered Time to production Response time from inquiry Annual purchase growth Functionality Process time to maturity Throughput time Processing time Break-even time	Are individuals able to work more quickly, more efficiently, and with higher quality, and are they able to decrease the learning curve because of the intervention?
Management	Employee retention Employee production Employee profitability Employee satisfaction Certifications Development plans implemented Budget goals met Work or department goals met Training costs per employee vs. overall employment dollars spent Safety goals met Personal goals aligned Employee survey Multirater 360 feedback Peer assessment	Did the intervention support managers in overseeing employees and improving on work goals?

Type of Measure	Potential Measure	Linkage to Intervention
Financial	Return-on-equity Combined ratio Business mix Operating income growth Sales per employee Expenses as a % of sales Inventory expense ROI Revenue generated Cost reduction vs. plan Margin vs. competition Expense ratio Loss ratio Shareholder value analysis Return-on-capital employed Quick acid ratio	Did the intervention support the improvement of the financial stability of the organization?
Technical	Technology adaptation Public perception of technical advantage Brand dominance Premium price on branded products Average annual purchase growth Investment in technology	Did the intervention support the increased technical capacity of the organization?
Marketing and sales	Revenue per employee Sales growth rate by segment Percentage revenue from new product, service, or customer Market share Improved delivery Innovative product creation New product revenue Cross-sell ratio Service error rate Brand image Public perception	Did the market position of the company improve as a result of the intervention?
Customer	Customer acquisition Market share Customer profitability Customer retention Customer satisfaction	Did the customer base grow, or did customer satisfaction increase as a result of the intervention?
Employees	Contractual responsiveness Problem resolution Functionality Timely submission of procedure Delivery time Safety incident rate Performance index Yield per employee Personal goals aligned Employee satisfaction survey	Are employees more satisfied with their jobs, and do they perform at a higher level as a result of the intervention?

(continued next page)

Table 7.4: Typical Business Measures *(continued)*

Type of Measure	Potential Measure	Linkage to Intervention
Innovation and creativity	Product launch success Product deployment Category dominance Improvements identified Suggestions for improvement	Did the intervention promote innovation and creativity?
Process	Time to develop new generation Process time to maturity Product or process performance index Process defects	Was a new process developed or a process improved on that improved communication, work conditions, employee satisfaction, customer satisfaction, business goals, or financial goals of the organization?

To accomplish these goals, you should choose measures that support the criteria identified in worksheet 7.2. Review each of the criteria listed against each measure that has been identified to complete a Level 4 evaluation. Measures not meeting all of the criteria should be reconsidered.

Worksheet 7.2: Level 4 Measure Criteria

Does the measure meet the criterion? Yes No	Level 4 Measure Criterion
☐ ☐	A direct cause-and-effect relationship can be identified between the content of the intervention and the impact on a measure. For example, a course for sales representatives provides a worksheet for use when responding to a request for proposals. This reduces the time to respond to customer requests and write proposals.
☐ ☐	The measure clearly is implicated in the objectives of the intervention. For example, the purpose of an intervention is to decrease call time for a customer representative.
☐ ☐	There is a linkage between the measure selected and a financial measure (or the measure is a financial measure). Most business results end up saving money or generating money. A measure that is not a financial measure is termed a leading indicator because it usually indicates that the money (a lagging indicator) will follow. For example, an increase in customer retention usually indicates that customers will continue to use the services and products, thereby generating revenue.
☐ ☐	The measure could be used to communicate to those using the intervention why transferring the intervention to the job is important to the company. For example, a safe environment is better for the employees because it reduces injuries and time away from the line.
☐ ☐	The measure is diagnostic in nature. If the measure does not change, it could be analyzed to determine if it was because the intervention had not worked or because there were other factors that affected the results. For example, a management program is implemented to increase employee satisfaction. But employee surveys don't indicate an increase in satisfaction. When investigated, it is discovered that there have been no pay increases for several years, and many employees are being given notice that they will be laid off without any benefits.

When the stakeholders request an intervention or decide that it is needed, they do so on the basis of some type of indicator. That indicator generally leads to the Level 4 measure. For example, a health maintenance organization (HMO) believed that a new employee orientation was needed. The culture of the HMO was complex, and when new employees joined, it took months for them to become oriented to the culture. Three "measures" were cited in the original project kickoff document: Orientation should 1) increase new employee satisfaction, 2) generate a faster time to proficiency, and 3) reduce calls to human resources for general process questions. All three of these are Level 4 measures.

It is recommended that you identify at least three measures when doing a Level 4 evaluation, but no more than five. Identifying three to five measures is recommended for Level 4 evaluation because they will yield the information needed and validating the information gathered will be easier. Three to four measures are about right; if you lose a measure (e.g., because it's biased or data are no longer available), you will still have enough measures to fall back on.

Building a High-Intensity Tool

A high-intensity Level 4 evaluation requires some form of statistical analysis such as normalization, correlation, regression, or another method that allows interpretation of the data in relation to other factors. For example, did the management program change the managers' overall behavior and consequently improve employee satisfaction, or was it the new stock compensation plan, or a combination of the two? This type of comparison is often termed data correlation. The purpose of data correlation is to determine if a relationship among the data exists and what it means.

Computer programs like SAS or SPSS can run a data correlation for an intervention. But it is up to the evaluator to identify the different factors that may have a significant correlation than the intervention. Tool 7.2 provides a list of questions to help you conduct interviews or focus groups with business partners, intervention participants, or stakeholders to identify what other factors may have influenced the data besides the intervention.

Return-on-Investment

Ensuring that the data was influenced by the intervention and not other factors usually is important when calculating return-on-investment. Consequently, ROI is typically thought of as a high-intensity Level 4 method. ROI is used to prove that the intervention either paid for itself or generated more financial benefit than costs. There are numerous ROI methods you can use when justifying or determining the payoff of a WLP intervention. Three of the most popular are as follows:

1. $\text{Benefit-to-Cost Ratio (BCR)} = \dfrac{\text{Program Benefits}}{\text{Program Costs}}$

The BCR is 1.0 when \$1 is returned for every \$1 invested. If the ratio is 0.85, it would mean that only \$.85 in benefits was gained for every dollar spent. In other words, the intervention lost money!

2. $\text{Return-on-Investment (ROI)} = \dfrac{\text{Program Benefits}}{\text{Program Costs}} \times 100$

When an intervention's ROI is 100 percent, for each \$1 invested \$1 was returned in net benefits. In other words, it paid for itself but made no additional benefit. Benefits and costs are usually calculated on an annual basis. For every percentage point above 100 percent, the intervention turned a profit. And for every percentage point below 100 percent, the intervention created a loss.

3. $\text{Break-even} = (\text{Program Benefits for First Year} \times \text{Life of Program in Years}) - \text{Program Costs}$

The break-even calculates how long it takes for the intervention to pay for itself. In other words, it tells how many years the intervention would need to be in place and being used before it paid for itself. This same formula is also called the *payback formula*. If an intervention takes longer than three years to break even, it will probably be obsolete before it does so.

Identifying measures and validating them prior to conducting the ROI study is important. Table 7.5 can help you determine the reliability of ROI measures. Six questions were asked in evaluating the reliability of the measures and reports:

1. Does the measure reflect program objectives?

2. Is the measure valued by top management?

3. Can the measure be computed for specific employees?

4. Is the measurement output available on a timely basis?

5. Can enough data be collected for reliable measurement?

6. Is the measure free from known bias?

Tool 7.2: Identifying Other Factors

We are conducting a study regarding (INSERT INTERVENTION TITLE) to determine its impact on the following business objectives:

(LIST OBJECTIVES HERE)

We ask that you are candid in your answers to the following questions, because the information will be very valuable to us as we plan other interventions, programs, or services.

1. To what extent do you think (INSERT NAME OF INTERVENTION) affected (INSERT NAME OF MEASURE):

   a. Not at all   b. 1-10%   c. 11-40%   d. 41-60%

   e. 61-80%   f. 80-100%   g. 100%

2. If you did not answer not at all to question 1, why do you think (INSERT NAME OF INTERVENTION) affected (INSERT NAME OF MEASURE), and what evidence do you have?

   _____

   _____

   _____

3. If you did not answer 100% to question 1, what other factors do you think might have influenced (INSERT NAME OF MEASURE)? Please be specific.

   _____

   _____

4. Why do you think those factors affected (INSERT NAME OF MEASURE)? What evidence do you have?

   _____

   _____

   _____

5. How might we validate this evidence (for example, with historical data, specific reports, other contacts)?

   _____

   _____

   _____

   _____

These questions each represent one point and are asked for each measure or report. For example, a highly reliable measure (call reports) received a 6, which means each question was answered with a yes response.

Level 4 evaluation can be rich in information for WLP. In linking the results to the intervention's original objectives, data can be derived about what other factors played a part in the results, how the intervention may have deviated from its original purpose, and other critical information. The downfall of Level 4 evaluation is that it can be time consuming and, depending how it is done, expensive.

Table 7.5: Determining ROI Measurement Reliability

Identified Potential Benefit	Projected ROI to Organization	Report or Measure	Impact on Business Driver	Reliability
Reduction in training time	Productivity increase	Productivity statistics	Customer	5
Reduction in travel costs	Expense reduction	Accounting reports	None	6
Reduction in errors	Customer satisfaction	Customer complaints	Customer	4
Reduction in return calls	Customer satisfaction	Call reports	Customer	6
Reduction in instructor time	Productivity increase	Productivity statistics	None	4
Increased sales	Revenue generation	Sales reports	Market share	5
Increased cross sales	Revenue generation	Sales reports	Market share	5
Reduction in returns	Cost reduction	Sales reports	Customer	5
Increased consistency	Customer satisfaction	Call reports	Customer	5
Deeper customer penetration	Increased loyalty	Sales reports	Customer	4
Fewer complaints	Customer satisfaction	Customer complaints	Customer	4
Employee certification	Consistency	Certification report	None	4

Chapter Summary

In this chapter, Level 4 (Results) was defined and criteria for when to use it presented. The levels of intensity for a Level 4 evaluation were introduced and how to build tools at low, moderate, and high intensity described. Finally, three methods for calculating return-on-investment were provided.

Discussion Questions

The following questions are provided to help you apply what you have learned in this chapter:

- What is Level 4 evaluation?

_____

_____

- When is Level 4 evaluation needed?

_____

_____

- What type of results information is needed in your organization?

  _____

  _____

- When would you use a low-intensity Level 4 tool?

  _____

  _____

- When would you use a moderate-intensity Level 4 tool?

  _____

  _____

- When would you use a high-intensity Level 4 tool?

  _____

  _____

- What are the three most popular ROI formulas?

  _____

  _____

References

American Society for Training & Development. *The 2000 ASTD State of the Industry Report*. Alexandria, VA: ASTD, 2000.

Kaplan, Robert, and Norton, David. *The Balanced Scorecard*. Boston: Harvard Business Press, 1996.

Developing Other Tools

Although Kirkpatrick's four levels of evaluation provide an in-depth view of the quality of the relationship with a customer (Kirkpatrick, 1994), sometimes none of them will meet the business need. This chapter introduces tools that may meet your evaluation needs better than those related to Kirkpatrick's four levels. Many of the tools discussed are more process-oriented than product-related. They support the WLP function because they typically provide feedback before a product is introduced to an audience. They provide "precustomer" quality control. You may face other evaluation issues that will need to be met through such means as

- benchmarking services and products against the competition; for example, an external consultant's work can be benchmarked against work provided by an internal service provider to enable your internal client to outsource without your assistance

- gathering specific information on instructor performance or on a product or service that includes expert and peer viewpoints

- completing an audit on a specific service or product set, such as an instructional audit.

These types of evaluations require a different set of tools. In this chapter the process for determining what (if any) other tools should be developed is described, along with

- case examples illustrating the use of other tools

- determining the need for other tools

- developing a benchmarking tool

- creating a comprehensive review

- designing and using audit tools.

The intent of this chapter is to provoke thought about how you can expand an evaluation strategy beyond Kirkpatrick's evaluation levels to meet business needs in creative and meaningful ways.

Case Examples

Case Example 1

Expert Brokerage provided training both for licensure and to meet regulatory requirements. The company was seen as a leader in the industry, and its management believed that any program or offering within the company should be seen as best in class. Knowing this was a strong value of the company, the WLP team agreed that it needed to ensure that its practices, processes, and products were seen as best practice.

The WLP team created a benchmarking tool and identified five companies in the entertainment, hospitality, delivery and shipping, financial services, and technology industries that were seen as best in class in providing WLP products and services. The WLP team then used the benchmarking data gathered from these companies to create standards for the design of any training product used for licensure or to meet regulatory needs. As a result, the WLP team saw an increase in the number of employees passing regulatory and licensure testing requirements, and the feedback from customers indicated that the training had improved.

Case Example 2

Tech Traders, a technology company, decided to implement an alternative to classroom training for its customer education. However, because most of its competitors still provided instructor-led classroom training, its managers wanted to ensure that the quality and consistency of the alternative training were top notch. They created a review committee of experts in the use and design of interventions using computer media (Web-based training, electronic performance support systems, computer-based training, and satellite training). The committee's members included instructional design experts, content experts, and experts in the design of user interface.

The committee used standardized worksheets to review each intervention (or part of an intervention, such as a training module) that contained rating statements for presentation, conversation (menu language), navigation, explanation, and content.

On the basis of the review, the committee discovered areas of improvement for the learning technology interventions, and Tech Traders implemented changes. The company realized the following as a result of the review process:

- increased proficiency
- increased productivity
- improved quality of output of those using the intervention
- greater satisfaction by users and their managers
- decreased learning time.

Determining the Need for Other Tools

Although Kirkpatrick's evaluation model assists managers in determining how or if WLP meets business needs, it does not always identify what must be done to improve WLP practices and processes. This is what the "other tools" assist in identifying and defining. Reaction sheets could provide an average score of 4.8 out of 5.0, but you still might not achieve a transfer to the job, and you wouldn't necessarily know why if only using Kirkpatrick's levels.

In addition, a missing link in many WLP evaluation strategies is a tactic to prevent mistakes before the customer uses the product or service. Optimally, one could evaluate the process itself to determine what needs adjustment or improvement without waiting for a result measure to indicate the need. There are a number of tools WLP professionals can use to obtain this type of information:

- performance management measurement tools such as performance reviews

- tools such as impact maps to review a process and determine where linkages are disjointed or missed

- standard evaluations of a product or service prior to offering to ensure that it meets certain standards or that it tracks variations to identify potential issues

- a benchmarking tool set to formally or informally compare particular products or processes against the competition or best practice companies

- expert or peer reviews that provide an opportunity for those with technical expertise to assess products, services, or processes from a professional viewpoint

- new instructor field reviews that provide in-depth performance evaluation to assist in building the "correct" instructional behaviors

- evaluating new media, content, or structure thoroughly to enhance the success of the course

- audits that methodically examine work, processes, products, or services against a pre-established set of criteria (e.g., industry standards, exception criteria) to appraise the merits or identify improvement opportunities.

The criteria listed in worksheet 8.1 can help you determine if one or more of these other tools are warranted for the evaluation strategy. Review each of the criteria and enter "yes" or "no" in column 1 for each item. The more "yes" responses you record, the greater the need for a WLP practices and processes evaluation component in your evaluation strategy.

Developing a Benchmarking Tool

Benchmarking can be a valuable skill for WLP professionals to learn. Data gathered from benchmarking provides a comparative analysis that underscores process and performance improvement. Benchmarking can be used as an evaluation tactic for WLP internal processes or as a service to WLP customers (table 8.1).

There are three types of benchmarking commonly used in WLP:

1. *Internal benchmarking* uses a standardized tool internally within WLP to benchmark the quality of services.

2. *Competitive benchmarking* provides specific competitor-to-competitor comparisons. WLP may benchmark its products, services, and processes to its business competitors or to its professional competitors in organizational development facilitation or instructional design.

3. *Functional benchmarking* compares similar functions within the same industry or industry leaders. An example of this is the *2000 ASTD State of the Industry Report* (ASTD, 2000).

Various methods and processes for benchmarking exist, but the five phases that are included in most are the following:

1. Phase 1: planning what to benchmark and how the data will be gathered

2. Phase 2: data collection

Worksheet 8.1: Criteria for Developing Other Tools

Yes	No	Criterion Question
☐	☐	Is there a demand for a measurement system to help WLP professionals gauge their progress?
☐	☐	Does the WLP team require a measurement system?
☐	☐	Is the WLP team responsible for a value-delivery process, and must it create measures to evaluate that process?
☐	☐	Does the WLP team want to participate in a goal-setting process and establish performance measures?
☐	☐	Does the team hire outside resources and require certain standards of performance from these resources?
☐	☐	Does the team need clear communication and remedial tactics to ensure commitment and buy-in to the strategy?
☐	☐	Are the WLP strategy, standards, and processes well understood and internalized?
☐	☐	Is it important to identify strategic operating issues prior to launching new media, products, or services?
☐	☐	Is it important to determine how WLP compares to the competition?
☐	☐	Does the organization value intellectual capital and seek to capture it, track it, and measure it?

Table 8.1: Processes That Can Benefit From Benchmarking as an Evaluation Tactic

WLP Internal Processes	Customer Processes
Design	Telephone answering standards
Media delivery	Employee attitude surveys
Alternative interventions development	Peer recognition practices
Instructor performance evaluation	Industry comparisons
Coaching and mentoring programs	Salary surveys
Succession planning	Customer service programs
Apprenticeship programs	Management incentive programs
Competency development and uses	Pay for performance programs

3. Phase 3: data analysis to make comparisons and gap analysis to identify performance improvement opportunities

4. Phase 4: reporting findings and recommending the goals for the process or service that is being benchmarked

5. Phase 5: developing action plans and implementing change.

You can collect benchmarking data from a variety of sources, such as

- studies conducted by professional organizations
- visits to companies that perform similar functions in a similar industry
- partnering relationships for exchanging benchmarking data
- conferences and other group environments to facilitate benchmarking
- the Internet and Web.

Information gathered during benchmarking can provide WLP with valuable statistics for decision making and goal setting. Worksheet 8.2 provides a worksheet listing the key indicators for WLP and the formulas for calculating the indicators. In columns 3 and 4, identify the study or organization that supplied the benchmarking data and enter the appropriate data for each indicator. For example, the statistics from an ASTD study could be entered in column 3, and in column 4 Company ABC's statistics may be listed. When data is unavailable for a specific indicator, note N/A (not available) in the appropriate cell.

Creating a Comprehensive Review Tool Set

As case example 2 relates, there are times when a more comprehensive review process pays off by providing specific feedback or recommendations for improvement. The most likely candidates for comprehensive evaluation tools are the following:

- a pilot of a new program, intervention, training course, or service
- a change in media offering—for example, use of Web-based training for the first time
- a quarterly or yearly review of instructors in the field
- a review of new instructors in the field
- a supplier review
- review of off-the-shelf materials or products

- any time complaints or concerns arise about a WLP product, service, or resource.

Worksheet 8.3 lists the components of the different types of a comprehensive review tool set. You can use this worksheet to determine which components to include in your specific review tool. In the first column the types of review are listed, and in the second column the components of each are listed. There is a place for notes in the third column specific to the case you are considering for a comprehensive review.

The people conducting a comprehensive review must be trained in techniques for observation, reviewing against criteria, documenting the review appropriately, and being somewhat invisible while conducting the review. Clear expectations for the review must be communicated to reviewers, the people being reviewed (if appropriate), and whoever else is participating in the review.

Another example of a comprehensive review is an instructor review process. Because many of our clients request a set of tools for an instructor review process, we've included an example of the Instructor Peer Analysis Tool and an example of an expert's analysis of the instructor's ability tool to convey how a comprehensive tool set might be incorporated or used in an organization. Tool 8.1 outlines criteria for evaluating peer instructors. When possible, give specific feedback that identifies both strengths and growth opportunities. Provide details, including what, how, and why.

You can use tool 8.2 to evaluate the instructor's ability to present the technical content appropriately and encourage learning. Again, when possible, provide specific feedback.

Designing and Using Audit Tools

Audit tools help you gather specific information about how to improve a system, product, or service. In most cases, designing an audit tool requires some type of benchmarking to identify best practices. However, in certain circumstances, standards are available and are used to complete the audit.

The steps in designing the audit worksheet are as follows:

1. Identify what it is that needs the audit review.

2. Determine how the rating sheet will work.

3. Gain agreement on what the actions will be for the services, programs, or products that do not meet the audit standards.

Worksheet 8.2: WLP Benchmarking Indicators

Benchmark Indicator	Calculation for Indicator	Study or Company 1	Study or Company 2
Level of spending on training	Total training dollars compared to other budget expenses (ranking) OR total training dollars divided by total organizational budget (%)		
Different media used for interventions	No. of and type of media used for interventions (ranking)		
Types of services outsourced	Listing of each service outsourced in order of no. of outsourcings or $ outsourced (ranking)		
Mandatory annual training time	Amount of required training time per employee (hours/days) OR amount of required training time per employee divided by total work time per employee (%)		
Percentage of programs that require coaching	No. of programs that require coaching processes divided by total no. of programs offered (%)		
No. of employees in apprenticeship training programs who are promoted	No. of employees promoted who participated in apprenticeship programs divided by total no. of employees in apprenticeship programs (%)		
Types of performance improvement programs offered	No. of listings of performance improvement programs offered by type (ranking)		
% of payroll spent on training	Total training expenditures divided by total company payroll (%)		
Training budget spent per employee	Total WLP expenditures divided by total employees trained ($)		
% of budget spent on learning technologies	Expenditures on learning technologies divided by total WLP budget (%)		
Average wage of trainers (calculated on full-time basis)	Factoring in part-time trainers, calculate hourly wage of each trainer and add together; divide the total no. by the no. of trainers (average hourly wage of trainers)		
% of budget spent on outsourcing	Total dollars paid to outside trainers or companies that provided training or services (e.g., design, competency development) to employees divided by total WLP budget (%)		
% of interventions based on skills and competencies	No. of interventions based on skills and competencies divided by total no. of WLP interventions (%)		

(continued next page)

Worksheet 8.2: WLP Benchmarking Indicators (continued)

Benchmark Indicator	Calculation for Indicator	Study or Company 1	Study or Company 2
% of interventions using alternative to classroom delivery methods	No. of interventions using alternative to classroom delivery methods divided by total no. of interventions (%)		
% of interventions with coaching strategies built in	No. of interventions with coaching strategies divided by no. of interventions (%)		
% of courses that have testing or learning evaluation mechanisms tied to certifications or licensure	No. of courses with testing or learning evaluation mechanisms tied to certifications or licensure divided by total course offerings (%)		
% of interventions using on-the-job training (OJT)	No. of interventions deemed OJT divided by total no. of interventions (%)		
% of basic skill (reading, writing, and math) offerings	No. of basic skill offerings (reading, writing, and math) divided by total no. of interventions (%)		
Use of learning practices (training resource center, employer-sponsored conference attendance, summer job programs, business-education partnerships)	Listing of each learning practice engaged in and compared to other companies (ranking)		
% of cross-training programs	Number of cross-training programs divided by total number of interventions (%)		

4. Establish the standards.

5. Pilot the worksheet.

Once your audit worksheet has been designed, you are ready to implement it. The following steps will guide your implementation:

1. Develop a communication vehicle for participants and managers that explains how audit data will be used and how feedback will be communicated.

2. Train auditors if necessary.

3. Conduct audit.

4. Collect and analyze data from audit.

5. Prepare reports from audit.

6. Determine follow-up actions as a result of the audit.

7. Where appropriate (instructor feedback, for example), conduct a fact-to-face specific feedback session.

8. Communicate findings and expected follow-up actions.

Tool 8.3 provides an example of an audit worksheet for a competency system. This worksheet has been used to compare criteria contributing to successful competency systems (best practices) with the components organizations have identified for inclusion in their desired competency systems. You can use the findings from this comparison to determine the components to include in your competency system, to validate your

Worksheet 8.3: Comprehensive Review Components

Type of Review	Components	Your Notes
Expert review	A subject matter expert reviews • if content presented is technically correct • if content is up to date • if content is sequentially correct • if content is complete	
Peer analysis	An individual in the same or similar job reviews • if professional standards are met or exceeded • what opportunities for improvement exist • if performance criteria are met or exceeded	
Design review	An expert in the field of design reviews • if content is written at appropriate level • if content is written for appropriate audience • if content is consistent • if objectives are clear • if content reflects objectives • if design enhances learning • if design provides a variety of learning methods • if design encourages implementation back on the job • if design has built in interaction and activities that are engaging and job relevant • if design supports outcomes and reinforces performance results	
Media review	An expert in the field of media reviews • if input devices (e.g., keyboard, mouse, voice recognition) match user capabilities • if environmental constraints have been considered • if navigational flow is appropriate and encourages learning • if functional keys are arranged in logical groups • if dialog boxes are user friendly • if design is fluent and intuitive	
Lab review	An expert in building and implementing labs and simulations reviews • if lab provides a variety of learning methods • if lab encourages implementation back on the job • if interaction is built in and if activities are engaging and job relevant • if lab design supports outcomes and reinforces performance results	
Management review	A senior manager reviews • strategic alignment of intervention or presentation • fit with organizational values and goals	

Tool 8.1: Instructor Peer Analysis

Reviewer: _____ Date _____

Course reviewed: _____ Number of participants: _____

Environmental constraints: _____

The instructor: _____	Yes	No	N/A
Managed time available for the course by controlling student distractions, activities, presentation, and discussion.	☐	☐	☐
Modified presentation, activities, and discussion for learner characteristics in specific group.	☐	☐	☐
Used feedback to motivate, reassure, encourage, and reward users.	☐	☐	☐
Used media effectively.	☐	☐	☐
Addressed problem learners discreetly and confidentially.	☐	☐	☐
Managed the group interaction and participation to ensure that all learners demonstrated respect for each others' ideas and concerns.	☐	☐	☐
Determined when and how to respond or when and how to redirect in the manner that was most appropriate for learners' needs.	☐	☐	☐
Demonstrated understanding of how adults acquire and use knowledge and skills in conjunction with learner differences.	☐	☐	☐
Demonstrated skill in applying the techniques and methods used for career development and implemented them correctly.	☐	☐	☐
Evaluated attainment of end-of-course objectives.	☐	☐	☐

Specific reviewer comments:

_____

_____

_____

_____

_____

_____

existing competency system components, and to identify constraints and or concerns before you implement or maintain a competency system. Competency system best practice criteria are listed in column 1. Record in column 2 the corresponding current or desired component of your system and note how it compares with best practice. In column 3, identify the constraints or concerns that surface from your comparison and note the action that should be taken to resolve the constraints or concerns.

Tool 8.2: Expert Analysis of Instructor's Ability to Convey Technical Content

Reviewer: _____   Date _____

Course reviewed: The Basics of Supervision   Number of participants: _____

Environmental constraints: _____

The instructor: _____	Yes	No	N/A
Explained the roles and responsibilities of supervisors to co-workers, employees, management, and customers.	☐	☐	☐
Described the dimensions of supervisory competencies.	☐	☐	☐
Introduced basic policies in supervising employees, such as job evaluation and salary administration.	☐	☐	☐
Presented the purchasing guidelines policy.	☐	☐	☐
Discussed labor-management relations and presented the complaints and grievances policy.	☐	☐	☐
Discussed the supervisor's role in productivity and quality improvement.	☐	☐	☐
Presented the flexibility a supervisor has available to encourage and motivate employees.	☐	☐	☐
Observed participants in role-plays and provided confrontation in confidential and thoughtful ways.	☐	☐	☐
Discussed methods and techniques of on-the-job training provided by supervisors.	☐	☐	☐
Evaluated attainment of end-of-course objectives for technical content.	☐	☐	☐

Specific reviewer comments:

_____

_____

_____

This tool can enable you to do the following:

- develop a high-quality competency system based on a comparison of a current or proposed competency system against external best practices

- identify opportunities for design of additional competency system components

- provide a starting place for discussing competency system design or maintenance

- evaluate a current competency system against best practices to identify quality improvement opportunities

- use a holistic framework for competency system development and implementation rather than focusing on a single purpose such as compensation.

You can also use audit tools to conduct a process evaluation, administration or logistics process evaluation, project planning process review, or media review.

Tool 8.3: Competency Audit

Competency System Best Practice Criterion	Current or Desired System	Identified Constraints or Actions
Each competency identifies the intensity or completeness of action.		
Each competency identifies the impact of the competency on the organization or the business results (i.e., rates competency against critical success of organization).		
Each competency identifies complexity of task and environmental or other impacts on task that are out of the employee's control.		
Unique dimensions are noted for each competency (e.g., ability to envision the future, to be innovative).		
System includes identification of linkage to other competencies.		
Thematic analysis is used to identify and group competencies.		
Performance criteria are identified and linked to competencies.		
Competency system allows for individualization by manager and employee.		
Competencies are linked directly to the organization's competitive strategy and industry positioning.		
Factors that affect the competencies (e.g., economic, political, environmental) are identified.		
The competencies are used to support selection, performance management, and reward systems.		
The competencies directly support human resource and developmental planning.		

Competency System Best Practice Criterion	Current or Desired System	Identified Constraints or Actions
Learning, certification, and other programs are based on the competencies.		
Competencies identify the work outcomes (quantitative standards) by identifying one or more of the following: • what is produced • results • objectives • goals • work product • results desired.		

SOURCE: Barksdale, Susan B., and Lund, Teri B. *How Does Your Organization's Competency System Compare With Best Practices? Team & Organization Sourcebook.* Edited by Mel Silberman. New York: McGraw-Hill, 1999.

Chapter Summary

This chapter introduced the concept of using other tools to expand on Kirkpatrick's four levels of evaluation to meet business needs in creative and meaningful ways. Determining the need for these other tools and ways to develop them was discussed. Specifically, how to develop tools for benchmarking, comprehensive reviews, and audits was demonstrated and samples provided.

Discussion Questions

The following questions are provided to help you apply what you learned in this chapter:

• Why is the discussion and presentation of "other tools" important to evaluation?

_____

_____

• When would you need to use a tool that is not a Level 1 to 4 tool?

_____

_____

• What is benchmarking, and when would it be needed in your organization?

_____

_____

- What is a comprehensive review, and when would it be needed in your organization?

  _____

  _____

- What is an audit, and when would it be needed in your organization?

  _____

  _____

References

American Society for Training & Development. *The 2000 ASTD State of the Industry Report.* Alexandria, VA: ASTD, 2000.

Kirkpatrick, Donald L. *Evaluating Training Programs.* San Francisco: Berrett-Koehler Publishers, 1994.

Piloting the Tools

*T*he purpose of the evaluation pilot is to verify that the evaluation tools developed as part of the evaluation strategy will provide the type of data that will lead the WLP team's improvement tactics. The tools should be piloted after the intervention to ensure that the intervention is stable prior to testing the evaluation tools. To do that you should use an already developed intervention (even if it is off-the-shelf) to evaluate the tools. For example, if you are using a Web-based evaluation tool set, you would identify a stable Web-based intervention and test the evaluation tool set on it.

The content of this chapter, which is focused on the evaluation pilot, includes

- case examples that illustrate the importance of a pilot
- defining the benefit of piloting the evaluation tools
- creating a pilot action plan
- tools for evaluating the evaluation tools
- roles and responsibilities for the pilot
- communicating the results of the pilot.

Case Examples

Case Example 1

ABBC Manufacturing had a well-developed set of competencies. However, the format of the competency system was not flexible, and the overall system needed to be updated to reflect changes in incentives, succession planning, and job rotation as well as be adaptable to a wide variety of jobs.

Before the overhaul of the organizational competency system was implemented, a competency audit was conducted. The tool used in the audit was created from benchmarking and best practices for competency systems used in high-tech industries.

The company used several individually designed competency systems to test the tool and compare the results against results that had been identified through other methods. It determined that the evaluation tool

was faster to use and more concise. The tool not only included the departmental feedback but also identified structural changes that would increase competency design productivity and use of the system by company managers.

Case Example 2

Secure Financial Company developed a set of Level 3 tools that could be used in evaluating the different WLP interventions. Prior to implementing the new evaluation tools, WLP piloted them with two courses—a supervisory instructor-led course and a technical Web-based training course. Both courses always received a great deal of feedback regarding the use of content back on the job.

The feedback from the pilot evaluations guided WLP in changing the directions and scoring mechanisms on the tools so they were more meaningful to those completing them. As a result, the tools took less time to complete and were seen as more beneficial when completed.

Benefits of Piloting Evaluation Tools

Piloting the evaluation tools allows you to "test drive" the tools and to identify bugs and potential improvements in the tools. It also separates the tools from design, media, or instruction, so the tools are stable for any intervention. This is important in making sure the pilot reflects changes needed in the evaluation tool and not the intervention. The following parameters for a successful pilot of evaluation tools will yield the greatest benefit when implementing the tools:

- The owners of the intervention are willing to provide the necessary resources to participate in the pilot of the evaluation tools. There is approximately a 5 percent overhead impact (e.g., schedule, cost, participant participation).
- The intervention is stable.
- The intervention is a good representation of the types of interventions the tools will be used to evaluate.

- The intervention is highly regarded.
- It is logical that if this intervention was being implemented, it would have this type of evaluation tool associated with it.
- The timing of the intervention (e.g., offering, availability) is within the parameters of when the evaluation tool will be implemented. In other words, there is time for a pilot.
- WLP can support the additional work involved in coordinating, modifying, and developing the necessary feedback and review forms for the evaluation tools.

Creating the Action Plan

Typically the pilot plan is included in the overall evaluation tool project plan. The pilot is often considered a milestone. The task list in worksheet 9.1 can assist you in setting up the pilot. Review the list and make any modifications specific to the tools being piloted. In column 2, record the date by which the action items should be completed. The person responsible for completing the action item is identified in column 3, and in column 4 the current status of the item is noted (this can also be used as a status report).

Evaluating the Evaluation Tool

The Tool Evaluation Sheet in tool 9.1 can be used to validate if the evaluation tools will provide the type of data that will lead the WLP improvement tactics. Anyone who will participate in the pilot evaluation should complete a Tool Evaluation Sheet. Once the sheets have been completed, the evaluation manager and WLP management analyze the results and determine the effectiveness of the evaluation tool, the modifications needed, and, ultimately, if the tool will become a standard for the WLP team.

Pilot Roles and Responsibilities

There are several roles in conducting a pilot of the evaluation tools. Each role has several important and unique responsibilities.

Evaluation Manager

The evaluation manager acts as the project manager and advisor during the implementation of the evaluation tools. The evaluation manager has the ultimate responsibility for completing the evaluation tool pilot and evaluating its effectiveness. He or she meets with WLP management and makes the final recommendations regarding the evaluation strategy and its tools. A primary vehicle for these recommendations will be the results from the pilot and the Tool Evaluation Sheets.

Client

The client needs to agree with and support the evaluation tools for his or her project and will need to complete the Tool Evaluation Sheet.

Instructor

If the intervention is instructor led, the instructor will need to complete the Tool Evaluation Sheet and ensure that all of the participants complete it as well. If client commitment can be gained and there are more than 50 instructors postpilot, it is recommended that a random population of 25 percent of the instructors be chosen. These instructors complete the Tool Evaluation Sheet for each class that they instruct. The data is reported and analyzed by instructor and then compared against the other instructors' data for common and contrary themes.

Pilot Participant

All participants will need to complete the Tool Evaluation Sheet.

Communicating Evaluation Tool Results

Once you have compiled and analyzed the results, you will need to communicate recommendations regarding the tools. The questions in worksheet 9.2 can be used to plan for communicating the recommendations.

Your evaluation report should include the following:

- purpose of the evaluation
- example of each tool
- findings, conclusions, and recommendations of the evaluation
- findings, conclusions, and recommendations for the tools.

The report should be no longer than four pages (excluding tool examples). In addition, a short summary of the key findings should be sent to all of the participants who used the tool with a note of thanks for the time they spent piloting the tool.

Worksheet 9.1: Pilot Action Plan

Action Item	Date	Person Responsible	Status
Prepilot action items			
Finalize the evaluation tools.			
Review pilot plan and surveys with the pilot team members.			
Identify pilot participants.			
Clarify pilot roles and actions for the evaluation tools.			
Notify participants and managers regarding the evaluation tools and their role in evaluating them.			
Meet with instructor (if intervention is instructor led) for pilot and introduce evaluation surveys. Discuss purpose of the evaluation tool pilot.			
Pilot tasks			
Introduce evaluation surveys to instructors and participants prior to beginning the intervention.			
Collect instructors' and participants' completed surveys at end of session.			
Answer any questions generated by the evaluation surveys.			
Postpilot tasks			
Collate and analyze pilot data from evaluation surveys.			
Present findings and recommendations to WLP management.			
Identify and take next steps to finalize evaluation tools and begin implementation.			

Tool 9.1: Tool Evaluation Sheet

Directions: As a part of your participation in testing this evaluation tool, please complete the following evaluation of the tool components. Rate each statement listed below on a scale of 0 to 5 (0 = did not apply, 1 = poor, 5 = excellent).

Name of tool: _____   Date: _____

Person completing evaluation: _____

    0 1 2 3 4 5   The overall content included in the tool

    0 1 2 3 4 5   The appropriateness of the tool in your work environment

    0 1 2 3 4 5   The usability of the tool within the intervention

    0 1 2 3 4 5   The value of this tool for improving this type of intervention

    0 1 2 3 4 5   The look and feel of the tool

    0 1 2 3 4 5   The overall helpfulness of the information the tool provided

    0 1 2 3 4 5   Your confidence in using the tool in the future

1. What did you like most about the tool?

    _____

    _____

    _____

2. What did you like least about the tool?

    _____

    _____

    _____

3. What of the information provided by the tool was most helpful? Why?

    _____

    _____

    _____

4. What was not helpful regarding the tool?

    _____

    _____

    _____

5. What would you do to improve the tool?

_____

_____

_____

6. What should ABSOLUTELY NOT CHANGE in the tool?

_____

_____

_____

7. Did the tool meet your expectations? How or why? Why not?

_____

_____

_____

8. Is there anything about the tool that you think would discourage its use for this type of intervention? What and why?

_____

_____

_____

9. Is there anything about the tool that you think would encourage its use for this type of intervention? What and why?

_____

_____

_____

10. Would you recommend using this tool on an ongoing basis? Why or why not?

_____

_____

_____

Worksheet 9.2: Communicating the Results of the Pilot

1. Were the results from the evaluation tool helpful? Why or why not? What needs to change?

   _____

   _____

2. Does the tool need to be redesigned and repiloted? Why or why not?

   _____

   _____

3. Is the tool relevant to the WLP team? Why or why not?

   _____

   _____

4. Is the tool presented in a manner appropriate to the user or audience? Why or why not?

   _____

   _____

5. Is the tool perceived as valuable? By whom?

   _____

   _____

6. Are the directions for the tool clear? Why or why not?

   _____

   _____

7. Is the vocabulary used in the tool appropriate? Why or why not?

   _____

   _____

8. Is anything missing? If so, what?

   _____

   _____

9. Will the tool fit within the culture?

   _____

   _____

10. Does the tool meet the needs and expectations of the WLP team, management, or client?

   _____

   _____

11. In your opinion, is the tool effective as an indicator of design strengths and improvement opportunities? Why or why not?

   _____

   _____

Chapter Summary

This chapter introduced how to pilot evaluation tools and discussed the benefits of conducting the pilot, how to plan the pilot, and who is responsible for what pilot actions. A tool for evaluating the evaluation tool was provided as well. Finally, how to communicate the results of the pilot was discussed.

Discussion Questions

The following questions are provided to help you apply what you learned in this chapter:

- Why is conducting a pilot for evaluation tools important to the overall evaluation?

   _____

   _____

- Who should be involved in an evaluation tool pilot in your organization?

   _____

   _____

- What is the best way to communicate the results of the pilot in your organization?

   _____

   _____

Implementing the Tools and Collecting Data

*T*he approach you use to introduce the tools and collect the data can either compromise the data or ensure that it is useful and beneficial to all parties involved. To assist you in successfully implementing the tools and collecting data, this chapter discusses the following topics:

- case examples illustrating how to implement evaluation tools and collect data
- communicating implementation of the tools and collection of data
- ensuring the quality of data collected
- potential unforeseen issues with implementation.

Case Examples

Case Example 1

Stellar Insurance Company's training and development department implemented a complicated evaluation strategy. It included a best practices study for instructional practices, establishment of instructional standards, and use of a reaction sheet to provide instructional feedback. As those responsible for the strategy began to look forward and analyze the type of data to be gathered, they realized that, although very important, it was one dimensional; the data included only the customers' initial perceptions. After all of the work involved in developing standards from best practices for instructors, they found that the instructors viewed the feedback from the reaction sheet as a "popularity contest."

The department expanded the evaluation study and implemented peer and expert reviews for each instructor. Management felt that this would provide a checks and balances system for the evaluation data and that the data would provide several views. The instructors felt the information provided from the overall evaluation was more accurate and fairer. As time went by, Stellar continued to improve the instructional evaluation system. All instructors are now certified within six months or no longer used.

Case Example 2

Software Developers Inc. used several certifications for its workers. It decided to include additional lab testing for certification. Unfortunately, the implementation of the change was not well thought out and, consequently, not well communicated. Workers found themselves with new job requirements and very little time to come up to speed. The workers became disgruntled and, in a tight labor market, began to seek new positions.

Through a quick save (relaxing the requirements and providing about a year for employees to get up to speed) and an expensive incentive program, the company was able to retain most of its workforce. But it was found that several of those who left first were some of the most promising employees. According to those who remained, this loss wasn't necessary; if the change had been communicated appropriately, it would have been well accepted.

Communicating and Gaining Commitment

As discussed in chapter 3, "Communicating and Gaining Commitment to the Strategy," communication and political savvy are key to your success in collecting the data needed. Much of the information presented in chapter 3 applies to the implementation step as well. The major difference is that at this stage the evaluation strategy is being moved into the environment itself and now directly affects your customers. How the implementation is handled reflects not only on the evaluation strategy, but also on the practices and credibility of WLP itself. Consequently, you should give some additional thought to who needs to be communicated with and what the message should be. Table 10.1 lists the potential communication audience and the contents of the messages they should receive.

Ensuring the Quality of the Data Collected

The quality of the data collected is critical. You can use worksheet 10.1 as a quality check during the pilot to review quality of the data collected, or you can use it periodically during and after implementation to identify data or measurement changes that may affect the quality of the data gathered. Review each of the standards in worksheet 10.1 to ensure that the measure used and the data gathered are of high quality and are useful for the business need.

Potential Implementation Issues

Most likely unforeseen issues will arise when implementing evaluation tools and collecting data. Each organization is unique, and the way an issue is handled must fit the culture and the business need. Dealing with unexpected issues involves 90 percent preparation and 10 percent perseverance. Worksheet 10.2 identifies potential issues related to implementing evaluation tools; all are examples that have surfaced in real projects more than once. Column 1 lists these issues, with room at the bottom to enter others you encounter. Using each issue as a discussion item, identify a strategy that would fit in your organization's culture and environment and still enable you to meet the business needs of the evaluation strategy and approach. Enter the actions proposed in column 2. When the worksheet is completed, you will have a problem-answer matrix to use when implementing evaluation tools and gathering data in your organization.

Table 10.1: Implementation Communication Considerations

Communication Audience	Message Content
Participants or users of intervention. This audience usually has the most concerns about how the information from Levels 1-4 will be used for performance (e.g., job rating and ranking, salaries). These concerns should be addressed first.	The information that will and will not be shared and how it will be used Expected results and why they are important Their role Business need that initiated the evaluation strategy Purpose and goals of evaluation Overview of tools, techniques, and process Overview of schedule and deliverables
Customers (if not users of intervention)	Impact on them Expected results and why they are important
Management	Expected results and why they are important Their role Business need that initiated evaluation strategy Purpose and goals of evaluation Overview of tools, techniques, and process Overview of schedule and deliverables
Report distribution list	How they should use the data Business need that initiated evaluation strategy Purpose and goals of evaluation Overview of tools, techniques, and process Overview of schedule and deliverables
Designers	How to support evaluation implementation Who to contact with specific questions Process for escalation of problems Purpose and goals of evaluation Overview of tools, techniques, and process Overview of schedule and deliverables

Communication Audience	Message Content
Systems support	Their role Who to contact with specific questions Process for escalation of problems Purpose and goals of evaluation Overview of tools, techniques, and process Overview of schedule and deliverables
Instructors and Web facilitators	How to support evaluation implementation Who to contact with specific questions Escalation of problems process Communication messages to other audiences Purpose and goals of evaluation Overview of tools, techniques, and process Overview of schedule and deliverables
Evaluators	Specific information regarding their tasks, deliverables, roles, and accountabilities in the evaluation implementation and collection of data Who to contact with specific questions Process for escalation of problems Communication messages to other audiences Purpose and goals of evaluation Details of tools, techniques, and process Details of schedule and deliverables
WLP department	How to support evaluation implementation Who to contact with specific questions Process for escalation of problems Communication messages for other audiences Purpose and goals of evaluation Overview of tools, techniques, and process Overview of schedule and deliverables

Worksheet 10.1: Data Standards

Meets Standard Yes	No	Data and Measurement Standard
❏	❏	Measure is in alignment with the business purpose. (The course content supports the measure. For example, a customer etiquette learning solution supports a customer satisfaction measure.)
❏	❏	The data collected for this measurement is not flawed and could be substantiated. (The data is not mixed with other data or flawed. For example, individual sales information is not mixed with group data and therefore inflated.)
❏	❏	The data is reliable. The data is collected in ways that will ensure that the information obtained is sufficiently reliable for its intended use. (For example, someone who is not biased is collecting the information.)
❏	❏	The data is valid. The data is collected in ways that guarantee that the interpretation is valid for the given use. (For example, a test is monitored to ensure the learner is the actual test-taker.)
❏	❏	The data is defensible. The data is collected in ways that uphold the accuracy and adequacy of the information collected. (For example, several instructors are polled, rather than a single instructor, to provide feedback on design materials.)
❏	❏	The data is collected in a way that the learner's rights and welfare are respected. (For example, test data is confidential and names are not attached to the results.)
❏	❏	There is "evaluator credibility"—the individuals responsible for collecting the data are seen as competent and objective so the findings achieve maximum credibility and acceptance of reporting.
❏	❏	Quantitative data is analyzed scientifically and statistically. The data is properly analyzed and controlled to ensure supportable interpretations.
❏	❏	Qualitative data is collected in a way that controls biases and preconceived ideas.
❏	❏	Content or thematic analysis is used to group and analyze the data accordingly.
❏	❏	Data shows patterns or indicators of a specific pattern.
❏	❏	Data follows statistical rules (if needed, data is time based or taken in sequence).
❏	❏	Data reflects performance against key business needs.
❏	❏	The collection of the data (e.g., who, what, when, how, tool used) is tracked, and there is an audit trail.
❏	❏	The data is cross-checked or balanced to identify and normalize variables that are found.

Worksheet 10.2: Issues Worksheet

Issue	Your Solution
You cannot get access to necessary data (e.g., costs, baseline, pretest).	
The intervention schedule has dragged, and baseline data needs to be normalized (e.g., a new incentive has been implemented since the baseline was done).	
You identify a corrupt data source (e.g., test items are invalid, a report thought to be objective is biased).	
The data collected does not make sense; there is an error in the collection process.	
A senior sponsor leaves the organization, and now evaluation is seen as less important.	
The data does not show trends or obvious similarities. (It is possible you may have to go out to a larger audience.)	
Participant or user cooperation is hard to get. For example, they won't return forms or attend focus groups.	

Other problems:

Chapter Summary

This chapter addressed how to implement the tools used to collect the data for an evaluation strategy or intervention. Case examples illustrating how to implement tools and collect data were provided, and how to communicate implementation of the tools for data collection was discussed. Also presented was how to ensure the quality of data and potential implementation issues.

Discussion Questions

The following questions are provided to help you apply what you learned in this chapter:

- Why is it important for you to communicate and gain commitment when implementing evaluation tools and collecting data?

  _____

  _____

- Identify one communication audience and the messages that would be important for that audience.

  _____

  _____

- What is one way you can ensure the quality of the data collected?

  _____

  _____

- What are two potential implementation issues that might occur in your organization?

  _____

  _____

Analyzing the Data

Whether you are doing research, completing a needs assessment, or investigating customer complaints, the principles of analyzing data do not necessarily change. The purpose for which you are doing the analysis must be considered and may place some constraints on the analysis, but the process usually is similar to that outlined in table 11.1.

This chapter focuses on the things you should consider when you analyze data from an evaluation tool. Specifically, this chapter includes

- case examples illustrating the considerations when analyzing evaluation data

- data analysis methods most commonly used with evaluation data
- documenting potential bias or inconsistencies in the data
- grouping evaluation data for analysis.

Case Examples

Case Example 1

Acme Financial Services implemented a new sales training system that included training and a new sales

Table 11.1: A Common Analysis Process

Process Step	Action to Be Taken
1	Determine the method of data analysis (e.g., content, thematic, quantitative).
2	Identify any bias that may affect the interpretation of the data or results.
3	Identify any preconceived ideas that may influence the findings.
4	Group the data (manually or using a computer system).
5	Test the data and determine inconsistencies or problems by forming hypotheses about the data and testing those hypotheses.
6	Tabulate the data.
7	Compare the findings with the raw data to identify any data defects or distortions.
8	Use the data analysis method to analyze the data.
9	Generate the findings.
10	Reach conclusions regarding the findings.
11	Make recommendations for the next steps based on the findings and conclusions.
12	Distribute the findings, conclusions, and recommendations.

incentive approach involving product prompts, potential customer product matches, and explanations of product features and benefits. The company wanted to determine to what extent the training effected an increase in targeted sales.

Acme's WLP group collected data in two ways: from focus groups and from a study using a control group and an experimental group. The control group had only the training and did not have access to the new system or the new incentive program.

The focus group data was analyzed using thematic analysis, and the control/experimental group data was analyzed using quantitative analysis. Bias was found in the control/experimental group data; some members of the experimental group moved to jobs in the control group to meet a critical business need, and the affected results were removed from the overall study to normalize the data.

The data findings demonstrated that the training alone contributed a 20 to 25 percent increase in sales, and other changes, among them the incentive program, contributed to the rest of the increase.

Case Example 2

Computing Hardware, which certified resellers (those licensed to sell, network, and repair its products), wanted to demonstrate to its reseller population that those who passed the tests it required for certification were more knowledgeable and skilled then those who either did not take the tests or did not pass them.

Using quantitative data analysis, the company compared back-on-the-job statistics for four measures: visit error rate, return visit for repair, sales completion, and net dollar-to-sales ratio. Those who scored 85 percent or better on the test performed 15 to 20 percent better in the four measures than those with lower scores and those who did not take the tests.

Data Analysis Methods

The type of data collected and the purpose of the evaluation determine which data analysis method will be used. The most common methods for data analysis are

- *Thematic analysis:* Data are grouped, or classified, by similar content or recurring theme. This method helps identify trends and validate similarities across the data. For example, a trend emerges that those who have used "bookmarking" (placeholders for frequently referenced information) in the EPSS are most likely to spend less time on the phone with a customer and to have higher customer satisfaction ratios. Data analyzed using thematic analysis typically is gathered through focus groups, surveys, or interviews.

- *Quantitative analysis:* Data is viewed scientifically and statistically. Often Excel, Access, a statistical analysis software application, or other software applications are used to assist in grouping and analyzing the data. The data is grouped and compiled, and percentages, counts, comparisons, and mathematical calculations are performed to create findings. For example, calculating sales ratios for those in a control group who had a low sales ratio versus sales ratios for those in an experimental group with a low sales ratio to see if those of the experimental group changed after training is a type of quantitative analysis.

- *Qualitative analysis:* This type of data analysis is very often descriptive. The data is typically collected through focus groups and interviews, although it can also come from other sources such as observer notes and survey comment areas. Often personal perspectives and direct quotations are noted, which can be quite wordy. The analysis identifies common themes and atypical data and categorizes data by specific topics.

- *Process analysis:* Data are gathered from observations and task analyses to analyze the flow of activity in a business process. Often the input, output, and process itself are evaluated. For example, are those who were trained in the sales training course using the process they were trained to use? Are they using it sequentially, as trained? Are the results from each step occurring as predicted?

Usually evaluation data lends itself to one type of data analysis more than another, but sometimes you can use two or three types of data analysis on data from one source. You can compute the cost savings from an intervention and then compare the steps taken in the process to see if each person who had cost savings followed the process as instructed. Table 11.2 identifies the sources of evaluation data best analyzed with each method.

Documenting Data Bias or Inconsistencies

As presented in chapter 10, flaws and unforeseen issues occur during data collection that need to be considered when analyzing the data. *Data bias* refers to ways in which the data could be prejudiced or corrupted, resulting in flawed data analysis. For example, if the individual analyzing the data has strong beliefs about the intervention being evaluated, these beliefs could influence the

Table 11.2: Common Data Analysis Methods for Evaluation Data

Method	Source of Data
Thematic	Level 1 comments Observation notes or comments Peer analysis notes or comments Focus groups Interviews Competitive research
Quantitative analysis	Level 1 (Reaction) Level 2 (Learning) Level 3 (Behavior/Transfer) Level 4 (Results) Benchmarking Best practice studies Audit of interventions Balanced scorecard measurement Certification review
Qualitative analysis	Level 1 comments Competitive research Best practice Benchmarking Any descriptive data gathered from individuals that includes quotes, comments, and the like Impact analysis Observation notes or comments Peer analysis notes or comments Focus groups Interviews Competitive research
Process analysis	Observation results Impact analysis Level 3 (Behavior/Transfer) Level 4 (Results) Balanced scorecard measures Performance analysis

way he or she conducts the analysis. In observations, sometimes raters see the people being evaluated as they see themselves and therefore rate them perfectly—the "halo effect." The halo effect also results in biased data. You can use Worksheet 11.1 to create an audit trail as well as to determine the impact of the data problem and what, if any, cautions need to be exercised.

Grouping Evaluation Data for Analysis

Grouping evaluation data often makes analysis easier, faster, and more consistent. Table 11.3 provides parameters for grouping data and identifies which data is best grouped in each way.

Worksheet 11.1: Data Bias or Inconsistency Worksheet

Collection Method	Bias Assessment Question	Response to Question
More vulnerable to bias: ___ Observation ___ Performance analysis ___ Level 1 (Reaction) ___ Peer analysis ___ Focus groups ___ Interviews **Less vulnerable to bias:** ___ Impact analysis ___ Competitive research ___ Best practice study ___ Balanced scorecard measures ___ Audit of interventions ___ Certification review ___ Level 2 (Learning) ___ Level 3 (Behavior/Transfer) ___ Level 4 (Results) Benchmarking	Who conducted or administered the methods identified in column 1? Is there any bias or rater error (e.g., halo effect)? Is there any potential bias or data corruption due to the collection method? If so, why, and to what degree? If a baseline was used, what changes or other factors need to be considered? Does the data need normalizing? If so, what are the factors and changes, and what is the impact on the data? Can these biases and data corruptions or inconsistencies be managed? Why or why not? Are any assumptions held regarding the data (e.g., expressed outcomes, expectations)? If so, what are they, and how can they be managed during the analysis? How can the raw data be tested for inconsistencies, corruption, and problems? Is the data contaminated? If so, how can the data be managed or reported to set expectations regarding the findings?	

Table 11.3: Grouping Evaluation Data

Data Grouping	Type of Data
Chronological arrangement: Arrange the data according to events in the order in which they happened or were observed.	Is helpful with observation data, job task analysis, and performance diary information and lends itself to process analysis.
Assimilation: Break the data into parts and then study any relationships to understand the whole.	Works well with most evaluation data and can be used with any of the data analysis methods.
Cause and effect: Perhaps one of the most powerful evaluation data grouping methods, cause and effect reviews the data for a cause and then a related effect. Once the causes and effects have been categorized, a clearer correlation or lack of correlation can be determined between intervention and result.	Works well with all data analysis methods.
Classification: Group the data by similarities.	Is helpful primarily in thematic and qualitative analysis.

Chapter Summary

This chapter discussed how to analyze the data collected using the evaluation tools and introduced an analysis process. Case examples illustrating how two companies analyzed data were presented, along with definitions of data analysis methods commonly used with evaluation data. The importance of documenting data bias and inconsistency was addressed. Finally, grouping data for analysis was discussed.

Discussion Questions

The following discussion questions are provided to assist you in applying what you learned in this chapter:

- What is the process used to analyze evaluation data?

  _____

  _____

- Describe one step in the data analysis process presented in this chapter.

  _____

  _____

- What is one of the most commonly used methods to analyze evaluation data?

  _____

  _____

- What type of data analysis would work in your organization?

  _____

  _____

- Why is it important to identify biases and inconsistencies in evaluation data?

  _____

  _____

Making Conclusions and Recommendations and Taking the Next Steps

Although the majority of the work is done at this point, the most important step is yet to come. Making conclusions and recommendations and taking the next steps is where the rubber meets the road. You will need to document the results of the evaluation, make decisions, and act on those decisions. Important considerations in this process are as follows:

- Who needs or will use this information?

- What information is actually needed, and how can it be conveyed?

- How will the information be used? What is the purpose of communicating the evaluation results?

- When and how often will this information be needed?

Following completion of this process, the data collected and analyzed will be in a format where the findings are clear, the conclusions are sensible, the recommendations are supported, and the next steps identified. This chapter includes the following topics:

- case examples illustrating how to make conclusions and recommendations and take the next steps

- linking the conclusions and recommendations back to the business need

- interpreting the data

- reporting the data

- initiating the action for the next steps.

Case Examples

Case Example 1

The WLP department of giftstogo.com, a small catalog and online product sales company, created a new orientation program for employees that was meant to reduce call time, increase sales and cross sales, and ensure that orders were taken correctly. The program was structured to include several types of interventions, including e-learning, instructor-led classes, and coaching. The WLP department presented this structure to the organization, and the WLP manager sold the structure based on the fact that it was cost-effective and would promote decreased time to proficiency back on the job.

A mixed Level 3 and 4 evaluation was decided on for the intervention strategy. The data was analyzed using a combination of quantitative and qualitative analysis. The findings demonstrated that, as a result of the multifaceted program, call time had been reduced, sales and cross sales increased, and fewer errors were made in order taking. In addition, not only was the new program more cost-effective than previous programs, but it also promoted decreased time to proficiency and decreased the coaching time supervisors spent in answering questions and providing quality assurance.

A final report identified the original business need, the intervention and its response to the business need, the evaluation approach, examples of the evaluation tools that were used, and a description of the data analysis and results. The recommended next steps were to begin to develop interventions with similar approaches for the other customer-focused and supplier-focused positions.

Case Example 2

Studerati, an automobile manufacturer, provided training to its licensed franchises on the repair of its cars. The program was optional, but the manufacturer found that when the franchises engaged in the program, overall costs to the manufacturer decreased for repairs, and car sales increased. Consequently, the overall program was seen as adding value. This program was WLP's primary set of deliverables. The program offered on-the-job kits and updates, instructor-led training, a minimal amount of computer-based training using simulations, laboratory training, and a certification program. The components of WLP's evaluation strategy included

- overall customer satisfaction with the products and content

- instructional quality and satisfaction

- logistical satisfaction (e.g., Were there phones available so business could be conducted during breaks?)

- satisfaction with administration and registration
- identification of new products that were needed but not currently offered.

These interventions were delivered regionally, and each region had a manager responsible for the delivery of the WLP products, although the actual products were consistent across regions.

The WLP department decided that the most beneficial method for implementing the evaluation strategy was to pilot the evaluation tools, gather the data, and then compile the reported findings in a manual that would include guidance on

- reading and interpreting the reports
- identifying findings from the reports
- drawing conclusions from the reports
- reporting regional findings to the desired audiences
- identifying and taking appropriate actions steps.

The pilot information provided the regional managers with templates for each report that included examples of how to use "real data" from the reports. This information helped the managers understand and interpret the data, sort out causes and consequences, and identify relationships among the data. This information enabled them to make conclusions and recommendations.

Linking to the Business Need

Beginning at the beginning is important when reporting evaluation findings, conclusions, and recommendations. What was the business need? What does the data say about how the intervention met the business need? What conclusions can be drawn from the data collected? And as a result of the findings and conclusions, what recommendations are made for the next action steps?

The linkage to the business need provides a sense of closure for the evaluation and substantiates the purpose of the evaluation and the effectiveness of the overall WLP strategy. It is also important to take responsibility for missed opportunities or problems, which increases WLP's reputation and credibility. The evaluation conclusions, both good and bad, will strengthen WLP's business partnership and demonstrate the group's willingness not only to be a team player but to contribute to overall business goals. You can use worksheet 12.1 to document the relationships between the data and the business need, draw conclusions about how effective the strategy components were in closing gaps, and make recommendations for the next steps.

Interpreting the Data

So how do you take the data that has been collected and analyzed and interpret it to provide meaningful information for a report reader? It is important when reporting evaluation results that you

- highlight the key findings
- confirm what is supported by the data
- identify misconceptions
- call attention to what may be less obvious
- draw attention to key points that may not be understood or known but are important to the business need.

One pitfall in interpreting the data, identifying findings, and generating conclusions is evaluator bias. When one has invested a great deal of effort to create or support evaluation, it is easy to be biased regarding the results. It takes a personal commitment to develop and evaluate products or services, and one hopes that the work will achieve the desired results. It is important, however, to follow these guidelines for good evaluation reporting:

- Be aware of your own biases and filter them from the findings, conclusions, and recommendations.
- Be open to what the findings say. Often "bad news" can provide creative opportunities for improvement.
- Generate options. As data is reviewed, begin to generate options. This will stimulate recommendations and next action steps.
- Review the data from multiple perspectives. Put the data in chronological order. Then group it according to key events. Review it from multiple settings and demographics, and do a cross-setting pattern analysis.
- If individuals are the primary focus of analysis, as in Levels 2 and 3, focus on their demographics and then interpret the data. For example, was there a difference in test scores between a manager and an associate?
- Organize the data by process. (For example, does the content support recruitment, and if yes, how?)
- Group the issues and compare the issues against other data findings.
- Analyze the data from the perspective of a case study.

Worksheet 12.1: Linking Business Need to the Findings

Original Business Need	Expected Intervention or Strategy Support	Key Findings	Conclusions	Recommendations
Meet or exceed quota	Product knowledge and sales process training strategy	Training did increase sales specialists' ability to meet quota. However, about six months after interventions, they begin to fall back and not follow through.	A session that is very focused on customer needs and problems and product matches would provide motivation to continue using acquired skills.	Conduct sales workshops every four months to motivate and speak to key customer data that is timely and highly focused and gathered by marketing.

- Be aware of and change your patterned ways of thinking. Change your habits on how you view data. (For example, if you always enter data into a spreadsheet and then sort it, sort it manually first and then enter it into the computer.)

- Make linkages. Evaluation is all about cause and effect. The data from an evaluation tool should have clear linkages to the business need, to the measures, to the content of an intervention, and to the practice of WLP. Identify and call out the linkages. If they are missing, this is an important finding too!

Reporting the Data

Evaluation findings usually are presented in one of two ways:

1. a one-time report describing what the problem was, what was done, how effective it was, and what is being done as follow-up

2. ongoing reports that are used to continually evaluate components, interventions, or practices and processes.

One-Time Reports

A one-time report usually includes the following sections:

- *Executive summary:* This is a brief overview of the entire report, explaining the basis for the evaluation and the significant conclusions and recommendations. It is designed for those who are too busy to read a detailed report or who need only the most important information. The executive summary is usually written last but appears first in the report for easy access.

- *Background information:* This describes why the evaluation was conducted and gives a general description of the WLP component, practice, product, service, or process being evaluated. The objectives of the evaluation are presented here, as well as information about what was being evaluated and what it consisted of (e.g., instructors, content, logistics). The extent of detail depends on the amount of information the report audience needs.

- *Evaluation methodology:* This outlines the components of the evaluation process and identifies the tools used. The purpose of the evaluation should be identified and a rationale for the evaluation design provided. (The evaluation methods and instruments should be provided as appendixes or exhibits.) Finally, any other useful information related to the design, timing, and execution of the evaluation should be included here.

- *Data collection and analysis:* This explains the methods used to collect the data. Usually samples of the data collected are presented in this section. Next, the data is presented with interpretations. If appropriate, the expected results are summarized, along with information about how certain you are in your convictions regarding the expected results.

- *Identified issues:* This describes any unexpected issues or environmental concerns that arose during the evaluation. Other factors that might have affected the results of the evaluation should also be spelled out in this section (e.g., the introduction of a new sales incentive program at about the same time as the new sales training program).

- *Evaluation results:* This summarizes the findings with charts, diagrams, tables, and other visual aids. The evaluation results section gives a complete picture of the evaluation's findings.

- *Conclusions and recommendations:* This presents the overall conclusions, with brief explanations for each, and a list of recommendations for changes, if appropriate, also with brief explanations for each. The conclusions and recommendations must be consistent with the findings.

- *Next steps:* This identifies the next steps that should be taken as a result of the evaluation and the people responsible for the actions related to the next steps. The importance of this section cannot be overemphasized, as it is often

difficult to motivate action on the recommendations. Outlining specifically what needs to happen, when, and by whom is a critical step in the success of an evaluation project.

You can use worksheet 12.2 when developing an evaluation report.

Ongoing Reports

When reporting on an ongoing basis, it is important to provide guidance to those who will be interpreting the reports; making conclusions, decisions, and recommendations; and initiating actions on the basis of the information. The content that should be provided for each report is listed in table 12.1.

When there are many reports, it is helpful to put together an Evaluation Reporting Guide that includes the following:

- a listing of the reports
- distribution information for the reports (who gets the reports, when they come out, the format of the reports)
- examples of the evaluation reports that will be provided
- examples of data interpretations from the reports
- accessing and using ad hoc reporting if it is available.

Initiating Action for the Next Steps

Finally, all the work involved in implementing an evaluation strategy is in vain if next steps are not taken to ensure improvement occurs. Worksheet 12.3 will help you plan for the next steps. This worksheet is used to track the next steps that result from the recommendations made from the evaluation of an intervention. List the recommendation in column 1, the next steps in column 2, the due dates in column 3, and the person responsible in the last column.

Worksheet 12.2: Evaluation Report Worksheet

Evaluation Report Section	Your Notes
Executive summary • purpose and objectives of evaluation • summary statement on methodology used • key findings • primary conclusions • recommendations for next steps	
Background information • purpose and objectives of evaluation • what was being evaluated • business linkage to the evaluation	
Evaluation methodology • methods and tools used to complete the evaluation • evaluation process steps • how the evaluation was conducted • current status of the evaluation (if parts of it are still in progress or if it is ongoing)	
Data collection and analysis • methods used in data collections • samples of the methods • type of analysis used	
Identified issues • issues discovered as a result of the evaluation • how and why the issues surfaced • other factors that influenced the results • if possible, the degree to which the other factors influenced the results	
Evaluation results • comparison of pre-post data (if appropriate) • key findings • charts, tables, or graphs depicting the results	
Conclusions and recommendations • overall conclusions • recommendations supported by findings • linkage to the business need	
Next steps • identified action items and next steps • identified accountability for each action item and next step • information from Next Steps Worksheet (worksheet 12.3)	

Table 12.1: Guidelines for Reporting Content

Content	Description
Name of report	What is report referred to as, or how can it be accessed using an online reporting system?
Purpose	How should the report be used? Why is the data being reported in the manner it is? Is it for developmental purposes only, performance management purposes, customer management, or other purpose?
How to access	How do you get access to the report? What are the instructions for accessing the report online? How can one be added to the distribution list?
Report layout	What information is provided in the report? What columns are in the report? What does the report look like? (This is a good place to provide a sample of the report.)
Report data	What data or information is reported in the report, and in what format (e.g., words, numbers, percentages)? Each type of data represented in the report should be called out and defined.
Data source	How was each type of data gathered (e.g., self-report, call monitoring system)?
Data interpretation	How is the data interpreted (e.g., percentage, ranking)?
Graphic capability	If the report is represented in words and numbers, can it be also provided in a graphic format? If so, how is this done or requested?
Frequency of report	How often is the report generated, and in what format (e.g., paper, online)? When is the report available (e.g., two weeks after a training program)?
Ad hoc reporting	Can ad hoc reports be generated from the data? If so, what data? How are the ad hoc reports generated, and in what format? Who should be contacted, or how does one generate an ad hoc report? From what system is the ad hoc reporting done (e.g., special reporting system like Focus or SAS)?
Person or group responsible	In case more information is needed or there are questions about the report or distribution problems, who is the contact?

Worksheet 12.3: Next Steps Worksheet

Recommendations from Evaluation	Next Steps	Due Date	Person Responsible
Marketing to identify problems each quarter and work with WLP to design a short workshop that addresses key problems and products that match those problems	Begin tracking needed data and developing a strategy to build these workshops in a timely and effective manner	2nd quarter	Marketing director WLP manager

Chapter Summary

This chapter addressed how to document the conclusions, recommendations, and next steps resulting from an analysis of evaluation data. In addition to case examples that illustrate the content of evaluation reports for two organizations, ways to link conclusions and recommendations back to the business need were also provided.

How to interpret the analyzed data and being aware of evaluator biases were discussed and the content of a typical evaluation report provided. Finally, how to identify and document next steps was addressed.

Discussion Questions

The following discussion questions are provided to help you apply what you learned in this chapter:

- Why is it important to link the conclusions and recommendations back to the business need?

- What is one action you can take to eliminate evaluator bias when writing an evaluation report?

- Which of the potential sections of an evaluation report would be appropriate to use in your organization?

  _____

  _____

- What are two topics that should be included in an ongoing Evaluation Reporting Guide?

  _____

  _____

Maintaining the Evaluation Strategy

The previous 12 chapters have illustrated the need for and power of evaluation strategies in strengthening WLP services, products, and credibility. However, if the strategy is not maintained, the results realized will quickly be undermined. It is important to maintain the strategy to ensure that what is being measured is important to the organization and future planning processes.

Revisiting the evaluation strategy is like having an annual physical, which reveals changes in your physical condition that warrant changes to your habits and perhaps different medical interventions. Changes to the organization, new performance needs, and even new trends in WLP should be reviewed and integrated into the evaluation strategy if necessary. Updating the evaluation strategy serves as a checkpoint to determine the changes that are necessary to the overall products and services offered by WLP practitioners. This chapter provides tools and practices that can help you revise the evaluation strategy.

Maintaining the evaluation strategy need not take a great deal of time—perhaps a week—because most of the information is available and awareness and understanding of evaluation have increased. To help minimize the time it takes to maintain an evaluation strategy, the following topics are included in this chapter:

- case examples illustrating how to maintain an evaluation strategy
- identifying triggers that indicate the need to update the strategy
- reviewing organizational changes that affect the evaluation strategy
- considering the results of the current strategy and determining if structural changes are needed
- incorporating new trends and practices in your WLP practice
- documenting the revisions.

Case Examples

Case Example 1

Technology Applications had structured its evaluation strategy to include a low-intensity Level 1 (Reaction) evaluation and a moderate-intensity Level 3 (Behavior/ Transfer) evaluation. The results from both were strong, and the WLP products and services were strengthened by the information obtained from the evaluation. When considering revisiting the evaluation strategy, the WLP manager intended to keep the strategy status quo. But when reviewing change triggers with management, she discovered that with the growth of business in the European marketplace, the company needed to become International Standards Organization (ISO) certified. To support this certification, a Level 2 (Testing) component was added to the strategy.

Case Example 2

Comprehensive Health Care included Level 1 and Level 2 components in its original evaluation strategy. When the data was gathered and analyzed, one of the conclusions (and the subject of subsequent recommendations) was that the design of the interventions was inconsistent. There was no consistency in how information was presented, on-the-job aids were difficult to use, and each deliverable from WLP (even if the media were identical) was set up differently. This made comparing deliverables difficult. As a result, WLP evaluators recommended that design standards be identified to ensure that each WLP deliverable was consistent. Therefore, Comprehensive modified its strategy to contain a set of best practice design standards and design evaluation tools.

Maintenance Triggers

Maintenance triggers consist of internal and external changes that may indicate the need to update the evaluation strategy.

External Triggers

External triggers are changes to an organization's structure, objectives, business drivers, and strategies. Changes in business drivers such as technology, competition, and customers will require a review of the evaluation strategy. A change in structure or organizational strategy will influence the focus of each level.

Internal Triggers

Internal triggers are changes that take place within WLP. A reorganization of the WLP department, for example, will have an impact on the evaluation strategy. For example, resources may become more readily available to assist with the strategy, or they may become scarcer. Changes in strategies, goals, or objectives affect the evaluation measures and potentially instruments for measurement. Finally, changes to systems or processes and procedures affect the evaluation measures and potentially instruments for measurement.

It is recommended that management review the evaluation strategy once every six months to determine if changes are required. The impact of change on the evaluation strategy is illustrated in table 13.1. Redefining the need, purpose, and objectives of the evaluation strategy will enable you to determine the changes required.

Reviewing Organizational Changes

In reviewing changes in your organization over the past two years, one or more of the following have likely significantly affected your organization's results, approaches, and strategies:

- technology
- customer sophistication
- marketing approaches
- global expansion
- lack of resource availability
- economy
- competitors
- organizational restructure.

In thinking about these changes, it is easy to see how quickly things change year to year. These changes, which are often responses to business drivers, create business need changes. Consequently, an evaluation strategy must change to meet the new business need. Typical organizational changes that affect an evaluation strategy are illustrated in worksheet 13.1. Column 1 lists potential organizational changes, and in column 2 you can identify how each change affects the current evaluation strategy and what maintenance might be needed.

Maintaining the Current Strategy

As was illustrated in case example 2, the results from the initial evaluation tools frequently indicate other areas of evaluation need. You can use the following list of discussion questions to use when conclusions and recommendations are being reviewed to determine if

Table 13.1: Impact of Change on the Evaluation Strategy

Area of Change	Definition and Example
Approach	There is a need for a different evaluation approach. For example, instead of or in addition to a Level 1 approach, there is a need for Level 3.
Measures	The expected information from the measurement data was not what was desired. The measure was not an indicator of the results. For example, it was originally believed that number of customer contacts (e.g., telephone calls, letters) was an adequate measure of ability to create a relationship with a customer, but it was later determined that the real indicator was the quality of contacts, not the quantity.
Methods	The method used to collect the data has changed. For example, a new report is available that was not available when the strategy was implemented.
Resources	A source is no longer available or a resource has become available. For example, a system is now available to track testing results.
Purpose	The need for evaluation has changed. For example, the original need was to ensure the quality of the instructors, but now most training is done with technology.

Worksheet 13.1: Organizational Changes Affecting an Evaluation Strategy

Organizational Change	Possible Impact on Evaluation Strategy
Business driver change	
Business need change	
Reorganization or structure change	
Change in competition or market	
Economic change	
Customer change	
Economic or financial change	
Product change	

data from the current tools indicates a need for other evaluation strategy approaches:

- Would any of the other methods (e.g., reaction sheet, testing, best practice survey) provide additional information that would be valuable in further improving the services, deliverables, and products offered by WLP? If so, which methods would be best?
- Was there a request for evaluation information that was not provided by the tools within the original strategy?
- Does the current strategy lack balance? If so, what other approaches would provide balance to the data collected?
- Was any of the data collected confusing? Would another approach clarify or validate the data? If so, what is the approach?
- As a result of implementing this evaluation strategy, is more evaluation being encouraged? If so, what approach would provide the best information for the business need?
- Is there a follow-up evaluation that would provide beneficial data to the organization? (For example, Level 2 was in the original evaluation strategy, and it now makes sense to do Level 3.)

You can use each of the questions provided to discuss the need for additional evaluation approaches as a part of the revised evaluation strategy.

New Trends in the WLP Profession

Just as organizations are experiencing frequent and rapid change, so is the WLP profession. A key component in maintaining an evaluation strategy is keeping abreast of new trends in the profession. Table 13.2 lists resources for identifying WLP professional trends and is a starting point for gaining information on what's new and how it might apply to evaluation.

Documenting the Revisions

There are two primary methods for documenting the revisions or maintenance to the strategy: 1) create an addendum or 2) rewrite the sections of the evaluation strategy that were affected. Of these two methods, the addendum is recommended because it provides an audit trail and history of the changes made to maintain the evaluation strategy. You can use worksheet 13.2 to document the maintenance of an evaluation strategy in an addendum.

Table 13.2: Resources That Identify WLP Professional Trends

Hosting Group	Site Address	Description of Contents
ASTD—American Society for Training & Development	http://www.astd.org	This site provides networking opportunities, research support, a marketplace with ASTD's products and services, information regarding conferences and membership, and links to other sites.
AECT—Association for Educational Communications and Technology	http://www.aect.org	This site provides links as well as two publications—*Tech Trends* and *Educational Technology Research and Development.*
Society of Human Resource Development	http://www.shrd.org	This site provides information regarding careers in human resources and links to information about leading-edge concepts. It also provides information about its journal *Human Resource Development Quarterly.*
ITTA—Information Technology Training Association	http://www.itta.org	This site provides current information about the information technology industry.
ISPI—International Society for Performance Improvement	http://www.ispi.org	This site is organized into three topics: information, publications, and professional services. There is also a job bank, a buyer's guide, and conference information.
ODnet	http://www.odnet.org	This site provides a resource directory with other sites of assessment tools, email discussion lists, a job exchange service, and an event calendar.
SALT—Society for Applied Learning Technology	http://www.salt.org	This site provides information for those in the field of instructional technology on interactive multimedia, performance support systems, and other learning technologies.
SHRM—Society for Human Resource Management	http://www.shrm.org	There is an online store, articles from *HR Magazine,* and white papers regarding compensation, management practices, benefits, safety, and health.
Amazon.com	http://www.amazon.com	This is an online bookstore with 28 subject rooms. Title, author, or ISBN number searches can be conducted. Bestsellers or books featured in the media also are listed here. The keyword "instructional design" yielded more than 100 titles.

Worksheet 13.2: Contents of an Evaluation Strategy Addendum

Addendum Components	Your Notes
Maintenance triggers: What is the reason the maintenance is needed? Identify the "what" that is forcing the need for maintenance. Establish how the former strategy is affected.	
Response to the need: What will be done to change the evaluation strategy? Will new tools be added? Will existing tools no longer be used? Will tools be changed?	
Business linkage: Identify if the business need has changed and, if so, how, why, and what the new need is.	
Detail the new tools: Just as was done in the original strategy, identify the approach, the tools that will be used, and the timetable for implementation.	
Identify the results: What is expected as a result of the evaluation? How will the results be used? Who will make the conclusions and recommendations from the data?	
Implementation plan: What is the implementation plan? Who will be responsible for the implementation? Which players or resources are needed for this revision to the strategy?	

Chapter Summary

How to maintain an evaluation strategy was the focus of this chapter. Case examples illustrated how maintenance was completed within two companies. Topics included the importance of maintenance, the internal and external changes that trigger the need for maintenance, how to review organizational changes and their impact on the strategy, the questions to ask to determine needed changes, and the components of an evaluation strategy addendum. To help you keep current on evaluation in WLP, resources for tracking professional trends were also provided.

Discussion Questions

The following questions are provided to help you apply what you learned in this chapter:

- Why is maintaining an evaluation strategy critical to its success?

- What is one external trigger for changes to the strategy?

  _____

  _____

- What is one internal trigger for changes to the strategy?

  _____

  _____

- What is one area of change that you think will occur in your organization?

  _____

  _____

- What is one component that would be included in your evaluation strategy addendum?

  _____

  _____

Appendix A: Index of Tables, Worksheets, Tools, and Figures

Chapter 2

Chapter 3

Chapter 4

Chapter 7

Chapter 12

Chapter 13

anchor—A description of performance that usually is listed in a series from the lowest level of expected performance to the highest level. The terms *performance anchors* and *behavioral-anchored statements* often are used synonymously.

audit—Comparison of a current practice or process against pre-established criteria.

audit of solution against standards—A method of evaluation that involves auditing a solution or training program to ensure that a process was followed or that pre-established criteria were met.

balanced scorecard—An evaluation method created by Robert Kaplan and David Norton that consists of four perspectives (customer, learning, business, and financial) and is used to evaluate effectiveness beyond financial measures.

baseline—A set of data that defines what the situation is at a certain point in time (usually before the intervention) and is compared with postimplementation results.

behavioral-anchored statements—Statements describing expected performance (listed from the lowest performance level to the highest) that are then used to evaluate actual performance.

benchmarking—The process of continually measuring and comparing an organization's business processes against business leaders or organizations identified as best in class to gain information that will help the organization improve its performance.

best in class—Outstanding process performance within an industry; often used synonymously with *best practice*.

best practices—Innovative or quality business practices identified during benchmarking studies and seen as contributing to improved performance.

bias—Ways in which the data could be prejudiced or corrupted, resulting in flawed data analysis. For example, if the data analyst has strong beliefs about the intervention being evaluated, these beliefs could influence the way the analysis is conducted and contaminate the data.

Bloom's taxonomy—A system created in 1956 by B.S. Bloom for describing in detail different levels of cognitive functioning so that the precision of tests of cognitive performance could be improved. The result of this extensive effort was a scheme that classifies cognitive processes into six types: knowledge, comprehension, application, analysis, synthesis, and evaluation.

business drivers—The internal and external factors that drive an organization's strategy and therefore its business and performance needs. An example of an external business driver is government; regulation or deregulation forces changes in competition or the overall business environment. An example of an internal business driver is technology; new innovations and technology create opportunities or needs for changes in information storage and processing.

business linkage—An evaluation strategy's connection to the organization's business goals, strategies, and performance indicators. If there is not a clear link, it is likely that the evaluation will not provide management with the information that is important to its operation.

business need—A requirement identified by an organization through examining business drivers and deter mining how the company needs to respond to an external or internal force. Examples of business needs include the need to increase competitive advantage, to increase sales, or to invent new products more quickly.

certification review—A method of evaluation that involves establishing certification criteria and measuring the extent to which a participant meets them.

communication plan—The plan used to communicate the evaluation strategy to management and other concerned parties.

data analysis—Analysis of the information collected during the evaluation using one of the following methods: thematic analysis, quantitative analysis, qualitative analysis, or process analysis. The analysis method used depends on the purpose of the evaluation and the type of data collected.

data collection—The gathering of the information required for the evaluation using the identified tools. An important part of collecting data is ensuring that it is of high quality and useable.

electronic performance support system—An electronic system that is used to provide job-related information to employees as they do their jobs.

evaluation report—Documentation of an evaluation study that includes the following sections: executive summary, background information, evaluation methodology, data collection and analysis, issues, results, conclusions and recommendations, and next steps.

evaluation strategy—A guideline and source for all evaluation efforts within an organization. It is described in a document that communicates the mission of evaluation; what is to be evaluated; how it will be evaluated; when and by whom it will be evaluated; and how it will be reported, maintained, and communicated.

expert review—An evaluation method that uses subject matter experts or process experts to observe or review results to ensure credibility and accuracy.

impact analysis—A method of evaluation that consists of using leading indicators to predict or validate lagging indicators and to identify causes and effects.

intellectual capital—An organization's intangible assets, such as knowledge, patents, brand names, and goodwill.

intensity—The depth and complexity of the evaluation, determined by many factors including time, resources, budget, data requirements, and decisions to be made from the data. Low intensity is predominantly perception driven, moderate intensity is statistical but qualitative, and high intensity is in-depth and exhaustive and includes evaluation of specific individuals' performance.

intervention—A specific event or system that is implemented to close a performance gap.

Kirkpatrick's four levels of evaluation—The most well-known and often applied method for evaluating WLP interventions. The four levels are as follows:

- Level 1 (Reaction): evaluation of participants' reactions to the intervention
- Level 2 (Learning): evaluation of participants' knowledge gains as a result of the intervention
- Level 3 (Behavior/Transfer): evaluation of participants' performance improvement back on the job
- Level 4 (Results): evaluation of the effect of the intervention on business results; the most widely used results measure is return-on-investment (ROI).

lagging indicators—Measures of end results such as ROI, cost reduction, profit margin, or revenue generation. Called *lagging* because the results happen over time and follow leading indictors.

leading indicators—Measures of performance, such as number of sales, that over time will have an impact on the end result or the financial result.

Likert scale—A 5- or 10-point rating scale used in evaluation that assigns numerical values to subjective data.

maintenance—Periodic updates to the evaluation strategy based on changes in the organization, new performance needs, and WLP trends.

measure—A unit that gauges progress or change against an established standard. Effective measures are identified from the organization's business drivers. Examples of measures are test scores (Level 2) and number of violations (Level 3).

measurement approach—A subset of an evaluation method—the way something (e.g., customer satisfaction, increase in sales) is measured. Examples of measurement approaches include tests, surveys, observations, or calculations of ROI.

methods—Ways to evaluate workplace learning and performance. Examples include benchmarking/best practices, Kirkpatrick's four levels, the balanced scorecard, performance audits, and impact analyses.

multirater 360 feedback system—A performance feedback approach that gathers information on one employee from managers, peers, employees, and often from outside consultants. It is called multirater 360 feedback because it reflects information about that employee from the total world of work.

mystery shopping—A structured program in which researchers pose as customers at banks, stores, or other organizations that have high customer contact. It uses a set of published measures to rate the performance of the service or sales personnel against established standards.

normalize—To conform or restore historical data to reflect current data so that it can be compared to determine the change realized from the solution or intervention.

owner (of the evaluation strategy)—An individual who is the champion of the evaluation strategy and who leads the evaluation effort. This person works with others to identify measures, build tools, and resolve political and other issues related to implementing an evaluation strategy. The owner ultimately is accountable for implementing the strategy and communicating its results to the business.

peer analysis—A type of evaluation method in which peers use agreed-on criteria to evaluate each others' work or results to identify strengths and opportunities for improvement.

performance audit—An evaluation method that tracks individual or organizational performance to plan. This can be done as part of a needs assessment or as part of an evaluation to see if transfer to the job has occurred and if individual or organizational performance has improved as expected.

performance gap—The difference between expected performance and current performance.

performance indicator—Variable that enables you to predict performance change so you can determine if the intervention will be successful.

performance need—How and to what extent performance needs to change to meet business needs and business drivers.

pilot—A test run of the evaluation tools developed as part of the evaluation strategy to ensure that they will provide the data that will lead WLP improvement tactics.

reaction sheet—A data collection instrument used to measure a participant's perception of an intervention; frequently used in Level 1 evaluation.

reliability—A characteristic of the data indicating to what extent it is accurate and reliable.

return-on-investment—The benefits and costs of a program; defined as a ratio or percentage.

scope—Parameters identifying what you will and will not evaluate, to what level of intensity, and to what extent.

scope creep—Expansion of the original focus of the strategy to include other things; can result in the project taking longer to complete and requiring additional resources.

six sigma—Structured application of the tools and techniques of quality management applied to a project to achieve strategic business results.

solution—A system or method to resolve a performance problem that typically is a combination of methods (such as a piece of courseware, a change in process, and an increase in incentives) that will result in a performance change or a new process or system.

sponsor—The executive or manager who is supporting the evaluation, who provides financial approval for it, and who navigates the political waters on its behalf.

stakeholders—The individuals who have the most to gain (or lose) from the business outcome of the solution and therefore the evaluation. These individuals also may use evaluation information to make business decisions.

tool—A job aid, guide, device, or instrument used to expedite the planning and implementing of an evaluation and to evaluate the results of a WLP intervention. An example of a Level 1 tool is a reaction sheet based on a Likert scale. An example of a Level 2 tool is a test based on behavioral-related anchors. An example of a Level 3 tool is a manager follow-up survey, and an example of a Level 4 tool is a results expectations survey. Other evaluation tools that do not fall under the four levels of evaluation include benchmarking, comprehensive review, and audit tools.

validation—Confirmation or corroboration of something, such as a performance need or an identified measure.

validity—A characteristic of the data collected indicating that it is the data required, and not something else.

Appendix C: Recommended Resources

Evaluation Practices

Bennis, W. *Organizing Genius.* Reading, MA: Addison-Wesley, 1997.

Brinkerhoff, R.O. *Achieving Results from Training.* San Francisco: Jossey-Bass, 1987.

Burns, W., Editor. *Performance Measurement, Evaluation, and Incentives.* Boston: Harvard Business School Press, 1992.

Edventure Holdings at http://www.edventure.com.

Edvinsson, L., and Malone, M.S. *Intellectual Capital: Realizing Your Company's True Value by Finding Its Hidden Brainpower.* New York: HarperCollins, 1997.

Evans, P., and Wurster, T. Strategy and the New Economics of Information. *Harvard Business Review,* September/October 1997.

Forbes Magazine at http://forbes.com.

Kaplan, R., and Norton, D. *The Balanced Scorecard.* Boston: Harvard Business Press, 1996.

Kirkpatrick, D. *Evaluating Training Programs: The Four Levels.* San Francisco: Berrett-Koehler, 1994.

Hagel, J., and Armstrong, A. *Net Gain.* Boston: Harvard Business Press, 1997.

Lev, B. The Old Rules No Longer Apply. *Forbes ASAP,* April 7, 1997.

Phillips, J., Editor. *Measuring Return on Investment.* Alexandria, VA: ASTD, 1994.

Robinson, D., and Robinson, J. *Training for Impact.* San Francisco: Jossey-Bass, 1989.

Stewart, T. *Intellectual Capital: The New Wealth of Organizations.* New York: Doubleday, 1997.

Thurow, L. Needed: A New System of Intellectual Property Rights. *Harvard Business Review,* September/October 1997.

Benchmarking and Best Practices

American Society for Training & Development. *The 2000 ASTD State of the Industry Report.* Alexandria, VA: ASTD, 2000.

ASTD Benchmarking Forum at http://www.astd.org.

Benchmarking Exchange at http://www.benchnet.com.

Inter-Agency Benchmarking and Best Practices Council at http://www.va.gov/fedsbest/index.htm.

International Benchmarking Clearinghouse at http://www.apqc.org.

Data Analysis

Davidson, F. *Principles of Statistical Data Handling.* Newbury Park, CA: Sage Publications, 1996.

Hedrick, T.E. *Applied Research Design.* Newbury Park, CA: Sage Publications, 1993.

Patton, M. *Qualitative Evaluation and Research Methods.* Newbury Park, CA: Sage Publications, 1990.

Sax, G. *Principles of Education and Measurement and Evaluation.* Belmont, CA: Wadsworth, 1989.

Van Maanen, J. *Qualitative Methodology.* Beverly Hills, CA: Sage Publications, 1983.

Yin, R. *Case Study Research: Design and Methods.* Newbury Park, CA: Sage Publications, 1989.

About the Authors

Susan Barksdale and **Teri Lund** have a combined total of 40 years of hands-on experience in workplace learning and performance and are recognized experts in the areas of competency system development, evaluation (including how to calculate ROI and how to value intellectual capital), strategic planning, needs assessment, and internal consulting. After partnering on shared projects for five years, they founded Strategic Assessment and Evaluation Associates, LLC, an entity through which they offer licensing agreements for their human performance technology models. These licensing agreements were developed in response to customer demand for the "how-to" behind their consulting projects. The models have proved successful in enabling clients to replicate the processes, methods, tools, and templates developed and tested by the authors over many years.

The authors are known for their practical approaches to WLP solutions and for translating complex theory into easy-to-understand applications. They have developed and implemented solutions for many organizations, including Hewlett-Packard, IDC (International Data Corporation), Intel, Microsoft, Allstate Insurance, NIKE, US Bank, The Capital Group Companies, Pacificorp, and TVA (the Tennessee Valley Authority).

Susan Barksdale has been a consultant to numerous large corporations for the past 12 years. Prior to this she managed training and consulting departments for two financial consulting firms. She holds both graduate and undergraduate degrees from the University of Wisconsin. Before entering the WLP field in 1979, she was a psychotherapist working in a major medical center and in private practice. Barksdale has taught a number of communication and behavior management courses at the University of Wisconsin-Milwaukee.

Teri Lund has been an external consultant for the past nine years. Previously she held training and performance improvement management positions for Barclays Bank, Kaiser Permanente, and Sealund and Associates. She has a bachelor of science degree in education from Montana State University and a master's degree in international business and finance from New York University. Lund has in-depth experience in implementing performance improvement strategies, such as computer-based and alternative delivery to classroom training, and is a recognized leader in the area of technology and its impact on learning and performance improvement.